Rome and Constantinople

Rome and Constantinople

Rewriting Roman History during Late Antiquity

Raymond Van Dam

BAYLOR UNIVERSITY PRESS

In 1975 Dr. E. Bud Edmondson of Longview, Texas, began an endowment fund at Baylor University to honor his father, Mr. Charles S. B. Edmondson. Dr. Edmondson's intent was to have the proceeds from the fund used to bring to the university outstanding historians who could synthesize, interpret, and communicate history in such a way as to make the past relevant to the present generation. Baylor University and the Waco community are grateful to Dr. Edmondson for his generosity in establishing the Charles Edmondson Historical Lectures.

Cover design by Cynthia Dunne, Blue Farm Graphics
Cover image is a medieval map of Constantinople and is in the public domain.
All interior maps were prepared by Ian Mladjov and used by permission.

Library of Congress Cataloging-in-Publication Data

Van Dam, Raymond.
  Rome and Constantinople : rewriting Roman history during late antiquity / Raymond Van Dam.
       p. cm. -- (Edmondson historical lectures ; 30)
  Includes bibliographical references and index.
  ISBN 978-1-60258-201-9 (cloth. : alk. paper)
  1. Rome--Historiography. 2. Byzantine Empire--Historiography. 3. Istanbul (Turkey)--Historiography. 4. Historians--Rome. 5. Historiography--Political aspects--Rome. 6. Historiography--Economic aspects--Rome. I. Title.
  DG205.V36 2010
  937'.09072--dc22
                                        2009046900

Printed in the United States of America on acid-free paper with a 30% pcw recycled content.

Contents

Map: The Roman World of Late Antiquity   vi–vii

Preface   ix

Introduction   1

1   Old Rome   5

2   New Rome   47

Bibliography   81

Index   95

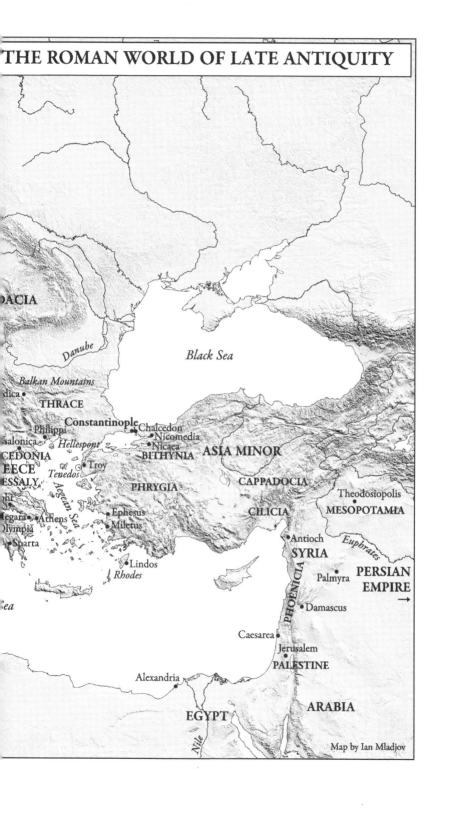

THE ROMAN WORLD OF LATE ANTIQUITY

ACIA

Danube

Black Sea

Balkan Mountains

dica •

THRACE

Philippi •

Constantinople • Chalcedon

salonica • • Nicomedia

• Nicaea

CEDONIA *Hellespont* **BITHYNIA** **ASIA MINOR**

EECE *Tenedos* • Troy

ESSALY

Aegean Sea **PHRYGIA** **CAPPADOCIA**

ht

egara • • Athens **CILICIA** Theodosiopolis •

lympia • Ephesus **MESOPOTAMIA**

• Sparta • Miletus

• Antioch *Euphrates*

SYRIA **PERSIAN**

• Lindos **EMPIRE**

Rhodes Palmyra • →

ea

• Damascus

Caesarea •

Jerusalem •

Alexandria • **PALESTINE**

ARABIA

EGYPT

Nile

Map by Ian Mladjov

Preface

The two chapters of this book are expanded versions of the Charles Edmondson Historical Lectures that I was honored to deliver at Baylor University in February 2009. I am most grateful to the department of history for its invitation, and to Jeffrey Hamilton, chair of the department, and all of the professors, both active and retired, for their hospitality. The informal meetings were as stimulating and enjoyable as the formal events, in particular talking about ancient studies with undergraduates over lunch and chatting with Alden Smith. I owe Ken Jones a special nod of appreciation for his assistance as a gracious and helpful host.

It is a complementary honor to have my lectures published by Baylor University Press in its Edmondson Historical Lectures series. Carey Newman, Elisabeth Wolfe, and Diane Smith have carefully guided the book through the process of publication. It is a pleasure to thank Ian Mladjov for designing and drawing the maps.

These chapters on Rome and Constantinople are also tributes to ongoing conversations about late antique studies with friends, both colleagues and students, at the University of Michigan. Paolo Squatriti inspired my interest in the symbolic significance of aspects of the Roman economy through his wonderfully innovative publications on medieval environmental history. It is my additional good fortune that my office is next door to his. Over the past few years Rob Chenault and Jon Arnold have written outstanding dissertations on Symmachus' Rome and Cassiodorus' Rome, and Adam Schor, Young Kim, and Nate Andrade on the eastern Roman Empire. Whether while arguing, bantering, or sharing, we professors learn the most from listening to our students.

Introduction

In late antiquity Rome had come to symbolize the grandeur and longevity of the Roman Empire, while Constantinople represented the increasing importance of the eastern Greek provinces and the northern frontiers. By then the destinies of the two imperial capitals seemed to be heading in opposite directions. Long ago during the reign of Augustus, Rome had become the largest city in the world; but after the Visigoths devastated the city in 410, it was repeatedly threatened by the Vandals, the Ostrogoths, and the Lombards in turn. In contrast, during the reign of Justinian in the mid-sixth century, Constantinople had become quite probably the largest city in the world. Rome recalled an impressive past, while Constantinople seemed to preview an impressive future.

Not surprisingly, modern scholars are similarly bedazzled by the remains of the great buildings and monuments in both cities and the ancient descriptions of their magnificence. The most stimulating books about Rome and Constantinople in late antiquity are Richard Krautheimer's *Rome: Profile of a City, 312–1308* and Gilbert Dagron's *Naissance d'une capitale: Constantinople et ses institutions de 330 à 451*. Krautheimer used the transformation of the old capital's monuments, including its churches, houses, statues, and frescoes, to chart the trajectory from imperial Rome to medieval papal Rome. Dagron used primarily literary texts, including orations, sermons, law codes, and histories, to discuss the roles of emperors, senators, prefects, churchmen, and ordinary residents in the initial making of a new capital. Dagron gave Constantinople a past by linking it with traditional Roman institutions and activities, while Krautheimer gave Rome a future by highlighting how it recovered from the neglect of late antiquity.

Neither book, however, was interested in the economic impact of supplying such large cities and their huge urban populations. In fact, even the recent impressive surveys of the Roman and Byzantine economies, *The Cambridge Economic History of the Greco-Roman World* and *The Economic History of Byzantium: From the Seventh through the Fifteenth Century*, ignore both the practical aspects of the supply system and its consequential impact in shaping economic behavior and ideas throughout the empire. This is a significant oversight. Because the ancient economy was so firmly embedded in cultural values and social relationships, Rome and Constantinople simultaneously posed practical problems and signified imperial rule. In fact, in many respects the logistics of provisioning were meant to facilitate the effectiveness of the symbolic value of the cities. The emblematic value of great size trumped the substantial difficulties of supply.

Dagron supplemented his book about the institutions of Constantinople with an equally important book about *Constantinople imaginaire*. This book focused on how the residents imagined the new capital, and in particular all the buildings, monuments, and statues, during the later Byzantine centuries. In the process of describing the fabric of the city, however, Byzantines also employed "Constantinople" as a symbolic medium for representing the nature of their emperorship and their empire. Rome in the early Roman Empire, and subsequently both Rome and Constantinople in the later empire, had served the same role as symbolic idioms. Both the residents of the capitals who consumed the supplies, and the provincials who paid taxes, were constantly thinking *about* the demands of Rome or Constantinople. At the same time, the great size and magnificent amenities of the capitals offered a medium through which Romans and Greeks could represent themselves and their communities. Both residents and provincials were also constantly thinking *with* the images of "Rome" or "Constantinople," in particular about the nature of imperial rule and the contours of empire.

The following two chapters try to connect the practicalities of supplying these two huge capitals with the hermeneutics of understanding the symbolism. In the Roman world very large cities were the consequences of ideological imperatives, rather than economic priorities. As a result, large urban populations, whether increasing or decreasing, required new histories. In the early Roman Empire the great size of Rome had been one warranty of its eternity. But as the size and importance of Rome diminished during late antiquity, historians had to rethink and rewrite the arc of its historical narrative. The magnificence of Rome's historical past then seemed out of step with the shabbiness of its current circumstances. The historical past of Constantinople likewise no longer corresponded to its current situation, but in the opposite direction. Constantinople needed a suitably illustrious past to match its recently enhanced size. Even as Rome needed a new narrative that could accommodate its unanticipated senility and possible demise, Constantinople needed a new narrative about its birth and formative adolescence.

Thinking about the great size of the capitals and the construction of these new histories can furthermore help us modern scholars understand the dynamics of the Roman Empire, both early and late. In the early empire the provisioning of Rome was an effective means for integrating the Mediterranean Sea, and in the later empire the provisioning of Constantinople had the same integrating effect in the eastern Mediterranean. The principles underlying the economic integration of these ancient Mediterranean empires were hence tribute exaction and redistribution, which both presupposed a firm commitment by the emperors to maintaining their capital cities. The emperors themselves had already realized that the symbolic value of very large capitals reinforced the political consequences. An economic landscape of demand and supply at the same time served as an imaginative mindscape of imperial power and domination. The commitment of emperors was hence not so much to Rome and Constantinople as large cities, as it was to *Rome imaginaire* and *Constantinople imaginaire* as powerful symbols.

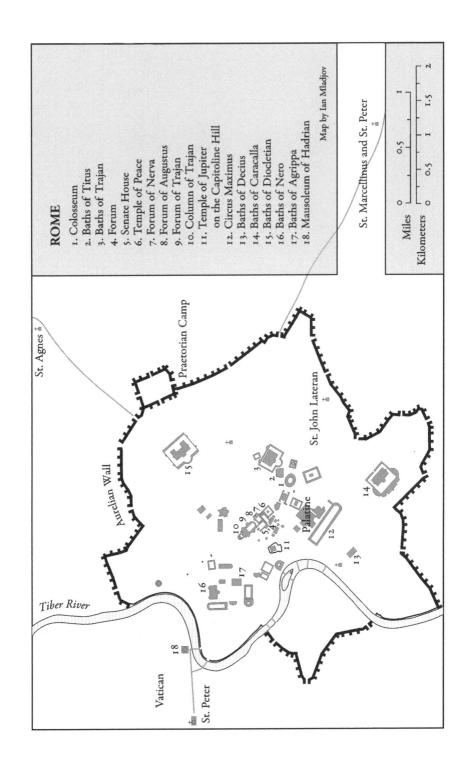

ROME

1. Colosseum
2. Baths of Titus
3. Baths of Trajan
4. Forum
5. Senate House
6. Temple of Peace
7. Forum of Nerva
8. Forum of Augustus
9. Forum of Trajan
10. Column of Trajan
11. Temple of Jupiter
    on the Capitoline Hill
12. Circus Maximus
13. Baths of Decius
14. Baths of Caracalla
15. Baths of Diocletian
16. Baths of Nero
17. Baths of Agrippa
18. Mausoleum of Hadrian

Map by Ian Mladjov

St. Marcellinus and St. Peter

Miles
Kilometers

0   0.5   1   1.5   2

St. Agnes

Praetorian Camp

Aurelian Wall

Tiber River

Vatican

St. Peter

St. John Lateran

Palatine

1

Old Rome

In the early Roman Empire, Rome is estimated to have had a population of about one million residents. Rome was hence far larger than any other city in the empire, in fact up to one hundred times larger than most other cities. Not only was imperial Rome an enormous city in the Roman world; it was also far larger than subsequent medieval and early modern European cities. In 1600 the combined population of the five largest cities in Europe (Naples, Paris, London, Venice, and Milan) still did not total one million residents. In 1750, on the verge of the Industrial Revolution, London had a population of 675,000 residents, and it finally reached one million residents only in the next century. Rome itself would not be this large again until the mid-twentieth century.[1]

Everything about imperial Rome was on a large scale. Even an ancient map of the city was large. The Marble Map, a schematic map of the city center clamped to a wall of the Temple of Peace

[1] For the populations of early modern European cities, see de Vries (1984) 270–78, with Woolf (1997) 6, on the population of Roman cities: "The rank-size curve for the Roman empire would thus be very much *steeper* than for early modern Europe."

and inscribed at a scale of 1 inch = 20 feet, was itself almost sixty feet wide and almost fifty feet high. The actual size of the city was overwhelming. The city's defensive wall, constructed initially in the later third century and subsequently remodeled, was about forty feet high and about twelve miles in circumference, enclosing an area of well over five square miles; the suburbs sprawled even farther. The substructure of underground drains was so vast that people went sailing in the huge tunnels. The monumental superstructure was even more impressive. Huge venues for entertainment surrounded the city's center, including the Colosseum, with seating for 50,000 spectators, and the Circus Maximus, with seating for up to perhaps 250,000 spectators. The grime was astounding. After his slaves promptly collected five tons of cobwebs, one emperor marveled at the greatness of Rome. Then there were all the residences, from lavish mansions to dingy tenements. Christian heretics once claimed that in heaven each deity occupied a different floor, as if in a large apartment building. According to a late Roman inventory, there were over 46,000 apartment buildings in the capital. Rome was apparently thousands of times larger than heaven.[2]

Urban Metabolism

Imperial Rome was certainly a grand city, and both residents and visitors from the provinces repeatedly remarked on its "marvelous

[2] For the Marble Map, from the reign of Septimius Severus in the early third century, see Wallace-Hadrill (2008) 301–12. Aurelian Wall: Coarelli (2007) 18–27. Sailing in drains: Cassiodorus, *Variae* 3.30.2, with Gowers (1995), on the rhetoric of sewers at Rome, and Aldrete (2007) 167–77. Cobwebs: *Historia Augusta, Heliogabalus* 26.6. Heretics: Tertullian, *Adversus Valentinianos* 7, referring to the Insula Felicula at Rome, to be identified with the Insula Felicles, located near the Circus Flaminius: *Curiosum* and *Notitia*, ed. Nordh (1949) 88. Number of *insulae*: *Curiosum* and *Notitia*, ed. Nordh (1949) 105; also Zachariah of Mitylene, *Historia ecclesiastica* 10.16, trans. Hamilton and Brooks (1899) 317, mentioning 46,603 "dwelling-houses"; with Hermansen (1978), concluding that there were in fact about 25,000 *insulae* in Rome; and Arce (1999), characterizing the *Curiosum* and *Notitia* as panegyrics, not administrative documents: "Estas cifras son . . . arbitrarias y fantásticas" (18).

immensity." In modern societies giant cities serve as hubs for networks of smaller cities, as gateways between regional systems and seaborne trade routes, as centers of exchange that produce their own goods and services for sale, as seats of political power and administration, and as leading sources of cultural and intellectual excitement. Imperial Rome did not readily fit into those categories. Its cultural influence often seemed inferior to the prestige of centers of high Greek culture such as Athens; even its reputation as a focus of Latin literature was carefully constructed as a partisan "selective representation." Its political influence was dependent largely on the presence of the emperor and his court, which initially was frequent but eventually became sporadic. Because the imperial administration was so small, there were no large acronymic bureaucracies or ministries headquartered at Rome.[3]

In fact, Rome was more of a burden than a benefit for the provinces. In our modern society cities with populations of one million or more residents are common. Throughout the world there are now over one hundred urbanized agglomerations with populations of three million or more residents, including at least twenty with populations of over ten million residents. Such huge concentrations of people are possible because of revolutionary improvements in production, productivity (of both land and labor), transportation, and distribution. In the ancient and medieval world, however, these factors were fundamentally constrained, and the size of cities reflected the limits on their provisioning. Reasonable assumptions about agricultural production and haulage efficiency over land routes suggest that in premodern times "market mechanisms could probably only support centres of 10,000 to 20,000 people from local resources." That was in fact about the size of almost all of the two thousand or so other

---

[3] Quotation about immensity from Edwards (1996) 108, in a discussion of ancient reactions to Rome. For Rome and Greek culture, note Swain (1996) 3: "The leaders of Greek intellectual life in the second sophistic period were part of a world that did not need Rome"; for Latin literature, see Woolf (2003) 221: "The City of Letters was not . . . a falsification of Rome, simply an exaggeration, or a selective representation."

cities in the Roman Empire. In contrast, Rome was most likely the first city ever in world history to reach a population of one million residents. Such a dense concentration of people required the importation of many resources from overseas for its sustenance and embellishment. As a result, the difficulties imposed by its vast appetite emphasize that early imperial Rome was an artificially outsized city that seemed to strain the capacity of the ancient economy.[4]

In the middle and late Republic warfare had contributed to enlarging the size of Rome, either because of fear or because of success. In the early third century B.C., the population of Rome may have already been between 150,000 and 200,000 residents. During the occupation of Italy by the Carthaginian general Hannibal its population had increased as the city served as a garrison. Subsequently Rome had become a refuge for impoverished Italian peasants who had lost their land and been displaced by the influx of slaves imported as captives from victorious overseas campaigns. By the end of the second century B.C., its population may have reached almost 400,000 residents. In the middle of the first century B.C., 320,000 male citizens were registered as recipients of the free doles of wheat; under the emperor Augustus the number seemed to stabilize at between 200,000 and 250,000 recipients. The amount of grain distributed to each privileged recipient was sufficient to support perhaps two people. Other residents purchased grain at reduced prices, while the huge number of slaves, perhaps up to thirty percent of the population, depended on their owners' generosity. On the basis of estimates concerning minimum subsistence requirements and deductions for lost and spoiled grain, in the early empire the amount of grain imported to Rome

---

[4] Quotation about market mechanisms from Landers (2003) 114; for the size of Roman cities, see Duncan-Jones (1982) 259–87. The short discussion here of the metabolism of ancient Rome could certainly be expanded to include consideration of additional inputs, such as energy (e.g., wood, charcoal, animals), and additional outputs, such as waste products (e.g., pollution, excrement, corpses); for application of this metabolic approach to medieval cities, see Hoffmann (2007).

each year was at least 220,000 tons, and most likely much more, perhaps up to twice as much.[5]

Collecting, transporting, storing, and distributing all this grain required a large infrastructure. Most of the grain came from Egypt, North Africa, and Sicily. Private shippers, under contract to the state, brought the grain for offloading at Puteoli on the Bay of Naples, or directly to ports at the mouth of the Tiber River. Transporting this much grain required at least one thousand shiploads each year, most arriving during the prime sailing season from April to September. Under the supervision of imperial officials, thousands of porters unloaded the ships and deposited the grain in huge warehouses. The grain was brought up the Tiber, over twenty miles, on special boats towed by teams of men or animals. At Rome it was again stored in large warehouses, before distribution as rations of grain or, in the later empire, as loaves of bread. Supporting this infrastructure of shippers, carriers, and haulers was its own infrastructure of shipbuilders, timber dealers, caulkers, ropemakers, stevedores, measurers and weighers, guards, and even divers to retrieve goods that fell overboard.[6]

[5] For discussions of population size and number of recipients, see Brunt (1971) 376–88, suggesting about 187,000 residents in ca. 270 B.C., about 375,000 residents in ca. 130 B.C., and 750,000 residents at the time of Augustus; Hopkins (1978) 96–98, suggesting between 800,000 and one million residents at the time of Augustus; Kolb (1995) 457, "In der Millionenstadt Rom"; Morley (1996) 33–39, suggesting 200,000 residents in ca. 200 B.C., rising to between 850,000 and one million at the time of Augustus; Christie (2006) 59, "approximately 900 000 from early imperial times through to the fourth century." In contrast, Storey (1997) uses comparative population densities to argue for a "Little Rome" with a maximum population of only 500,000 residents. For discussions of the amount of grain imported annually, see Rickman (1980) 231–35, 40 million *modii*, i.e., almost 300,000 tons; Garnsey and Saller (1987) 85, "within the range of around 200,000 to 400,000 tonnes"; Mattingly and Aldrete (2000) 154, minimum of 237,000 metric tons; Harris (2000) 717, "more than 250,000 tonnes."

[6] Mattingly and Aldrete (2000) 154, calculating a minimum of 948 shiploads of wheat each year, 104 shiploads of olive oil, and 640 shiploads of wine. Note that many discussions of the level of taxation in the Roman imperial economy do not take into account the hidden supplementary costs of maintaining

Grain was not the only food imported into Rome. The other two primary components of a Mediterranean diet were olive oil and wine, which at minimum estimated levels for one million residents together required another 750 shiploads each year. The primary sources for olive oil included North Africa and southern Spain, and for wine, southern Gaul, eastern Spain, and Italy itself. Initially oil and wine were imported for sale in the markets of Rome at low prices. In the later second century A.D., however, emperors began to supply free olive oil, and in the later third century they added pork and perhaps wine to the dole. Thereafter ordinary people at the capital might be known with the satirical nicknames of "Pot Belly," "Glutton," "Sausage," and "Piglet." The food supply of Rome had become, literally, pork barrel politics.[7]

Emperors also supplied water to the city. The first aqueduct had been built already in the late fourth century B.C., at public expense. Subsequent aqueducts memorialized military victories. The next aqueduct was funded with booty captured from a foreign invader; the construction of another aqueduct followed soon after the final defeat of Carthage in 146 B.C. As an indication of the increasing wealth of the Roman state, these early aqueducts became progressively longer. The first one extended only about eleven miles, the next one forty miles, and the next one almost sixty miles. Augustus and his agents repaired these early aqueducts and added more. So did subsequent emperors, at their own expense. The water apparently flowed nonstop, day and night, "as

---

Rome, including labor, transportation, and the supply of non-food commodities such as wood for heating the baths: see Tengström (1974) 89, on the "considerable amount of labour" required to produce, transport, and store grain, and Lo Cascio (2007) 624: "even if . . . taxes in kind and rent in kind . . . made it unnecessary for the state to purchase grain, the costs of transport . . . had to be borne by the state."

[7] *Historia Augusta, Severus* 18.3, oil, *Aurelianus* 35.2, pork, 48.1–4, wine. Nicknames: Ammianus Marcellinus, *Res gestae* 28.4.28, "Semicupae . . . cum Gluturino . . . , et Lucanicus cum Porclaca," with Barnish (1987), discussing the supply of pork, and Sirks (1991) 361–94, on the distribution of meat, olive oil, and wine.

a particular sign of richness and a high standard of living." Even though a considerable amount of this water was diverted to the needs of emperors and aristocratic landowners, by the later first century A.D. the nine aqueducts delivered, for a population of one million residents, an average of over fifty gallons per person each day. By the fourth century nineteen aqueducts were supplying the city.[8]

In the city this water was used for drinking, bathing, and flushing sewage. The aqueducts fed well over one thousand public fountains and about nine hundred public baths. The early emperors and their agents added several enormous imperial baths, including the Baths of Agrippa, the Baths of Nero, the Baths of Titus, the Baths of Trajan, and the Baths of Decius. Some were especially lavish. The Baths of Caracalla, constructed in the early third century east of the Circus Maximus, covered almost twenty-five acres. In addition to offering a hot room, a cold room, a swimming pool, and exercise courts, these Baths were decorated with marble columns and wall veneers, floor mosaics, friezes, and sculptures. Constructing these Baths involved importing tons of stone blocks, marble panels, bricks, timber, lime for mortar, and lead clamps and pipes, as well as building a new branchline from an aqueduct. Almost ten thousand laborers were required every day during the four years of the main construction. The annual construction costs of the Baths of Caracalla were perhaps one-third or one-quarter of the value of the grain imported to Rome each year. One visitor to Rome compared the size of these bathing complexes to "the scale of provinces." In the medieval period cartographers

---

[8] Diodorus Siculus, *Bibliotheca historica* 20.36.1, public funds for Aqua Appia; Frontinus, *De aquis urbis Romae* 1.6, booty from Pyrrhus for Aqua Anio Vetus, 7, Aqua Marcia. Quotation about richness from Bruun (1991) 112. Amount of water: de Kleijn (2001) 69, maximum of 635 million liters per day supplied by aqueducts in 97, 71, one-third of this amount available to public in Rome; for other estimates, see Bruun (1991) 101–4, only 67 liters (= ca. 16 gallons) per person each day, and Dodge (2000) 184–85, up to 300 gallons per person each day, in an excellent survey of the water supply at Rome. Nineteen aqueducts: *Curiosum* and *Notitia*, ed. Nordh (1949) 101–2.

were misled by the size and extravagance of the Baths of Caracalla to label this large complex as the imperial palace.[9]

To complement the supplies of food the emperors also organized and funded entertainments. Bread and circuses: before the shows could start, the emperors had to construct the arenas, including huge amphitheaters, such as the Colosseum, and even larger race tracks, such as the Circus Maximus. The entertainments consisted of games featuring horse and chariot races, gladiator fights, or wild beast hunts. The emperors owned sprawling ranches in the provinces, and horses from Spain and Cappadocia (in central Asia Minor) were especially famous in the races at Rome. Gladiators had to be trained and maintained; sometimes the fighters were simply barbarian captives from frontier battles. The supply of exotic animals was a considerable enterprise in outlying provinces. Professional hunters trapped wild animals, including lions and tigers, in pits or nets, transferred them to cages, and transported them to the coast. Along the way cities were expected to provide supplies for the hunters and the animals. On the ships that carried the animals to Italy "the crew was terrified at its own cargo." In Italy some of the animals might be kept in menageries for display, but most were held in stockyards in anticipation of their use in the games. As with the grain imported from the provinces, Rome seemed to have first claim on these exotic animals, in particular lions. Even when the emperors conceded permission to kill rogue lions in the provinces, they did so with a sigh of reluctance: "of necessity the safety of our provincials takes priority over our entertainment." Gladiators, racehorses, and wild animals were all imported from the provinces and frontier regions to be viewed and consumed at Rome. When the emperor Septimius Severus once released seven hundred exotic animals in the arena, including

---

[9] Baths of Caracalla: see DeLaine (1997) 41, medieval maps, 193, work force, 220, costs, in an outstanding examination of the construction and expenses of a large public building in imperial Rome. Size: Ammianus Marcellinus, *Res gestae* 16.10.14, "lavacra in modum provinciarum exstructa."

lions, bears, and ostriches, the people watched them first running around together, and then being systematically slaughtered. Long after the military campaigns had ended, the fighting continued, but now in the controlled space of arenas at Rome.[10]

Not everything at Rome was free, however. Residents had to pay rent and purchase clothes and services, and even the recipients of the grain doles supplemented their diets by purchasing additional food, such as the fruits and vegetables grown in central Italy. At Rome there were many opportunities for employment, in providing personal services, in the transportation of grain and other materials, in construction, or in the manufacture of bricks, tiles, and other goods for local use. Some of these workshops were owned or funded by wealthy aristocrats. But the wages for many of these jobs came from the state treasury, which was filled by taxes from provincials, or the emperor's treasury, which was filled by rents from overseas imperial estates. Many of the people of Rome hence lived off revenues from the provinces twice over, both as taxes paid to them as wages that they used to buy imported and locally produced goods, and as grain and other foodstuffs imported directly from the provinces and distributed free or at reduced prices.[11]

---

[10] Racehorses from Spain and Cappadocia: *Codex Theodosianus* 15.10.1, with Van Dam (2002) 23, 66, 111–12, on imperial ranches in Cappadocia. Supplies for animals: *Codex Theodosianus* 15.11.2, issued in 417; with Jennison (1937) 137–53. According to *Anthologia Graeca* 7.626, emperors captured so many lions in Libya that the plains could serve as pastures; Bertrandy (1987) compared the Roman harvesting of animals from North Africa to the hunting of buffalo to near extinction in the American plains: "on reste cependant stupéfait par les quantités énormes d'animaux qui ont été importée d'Afrique vers l'Italie" (234). Crew: Claudian, *De consulatu Stilichonis* 3.327. Safety: *Codex Theodosianus* 15.11.1, issued in 414. Septimius Severus' hunt, perhaps to celebrate the tenth anniversary of his reign in 202: Dio, *Historiae Romanae* 76.1.4–5.

[11] For diversification in central Italy away from the production of grain to the production of vegetables, fruit, and wine, see Morley (1996) 83–142. For jobs at Rome, see Treggiari (1980), and Brunt (1980) 98, "the grain dole was not enough, and the provision of employment from public funds remained important." DeLaine (2000) 135–36, estimates that at Rome the "percentage of

Such a large population could be sustained only through constant immigration. As in other large preindustrial cities, mortality rates were significantly higher in Rome than in the countryside. Diseases such as malaria and tuberculosis were endemic, and the lack of effective sanitation was quite unhealthy. The population of Rome could not reproduce itself through local births alone. Instead, thousands of people were "imported," perhaps 1 percent of the city's total population or as many as 10,000 migrants each year at the height of its size. In the early Roman Empire the overall population of the empire is generally assumed to have been more or less stationary, variously estimated between 50 and 70 million subjects. Sustaining the population of the capital at a stationary level, however, would have required a surplus of births each year among provincials. In a regime of high mortality rates, the average life expectancy at birth in the Roman world was approximately twenty-five years, and less than 50 percent of babies lived to age twenty. Generating 10,000 migrants each year, each about twenty years old, required almost 22,000 births. If the surplus of births among Italians and provincials was 3 per 1,000, then the maintenance of Rome's population was absorbing the surplus of about 7.3 million subjects; but if that surplus of births was only 1 per 1,000, then Rome was absorbing the surplus of 22 million subjects, representing one-third or more of the empire's entire population. The epitaph for one merchant from Phrygia in Asia Minor noted that he had sailed to Italy seventy-two times. The wonder is not that he had visited Italy and Rome so often. The surprise is that he had returned to his hometown each time. Many visitors to Rome had stayed to become residents.[12]

---

the population involved in the building industry was . . . perhaps 15% of the adult males." After surveying the economic activities of both men and women at Rome, Kolb (1995) 495, concludes that "Die Stadtrömer waren . . . keine untätigen Parasiten," but he does not discuss the sources of their wages.

[12] Migrants: Morley (1996) 46, "steady annual import of slaves and migrants," (2003) 150, "perhaps ten thousand or more, every year." Diseases: Scheidel (2003) 158, "the capital of infection and disease." Sanitation: Scobie (1986). Stationary population of empire: Parkin (1992) 84, although Frier

In the early Roman Empire supplying food and other resources to Rome was one large burden on provincials; another, of course, was supplying the hundreds of thousands of soldiers now stationed permanently along the frontiers. The massive burden of supplying Rome had the effect of stimulating agricultural production in the provinces, especially the provinces surrounding the western Mediterranean. In North Africa in particular, the amount of land devoted to the production of grain and olive oil increased considerably. This expansion of agricultural output was certainly "a direct result of public policies." But it was not the most important objective of those policies, or even an intended objective. Instead, the supply of Rome (and the army) came first. The expansion of agriculture, even if it may be considered beneficial for the provincials, was a consequence of the need to supply the capital. Once the emperors decided to underwrite the large size of Rome, provincials had to produce more to supply it.[13]

Rome was a classic example of a consumer city that did not pay for its needs through manufacture, trade, or reciprocal

---

(2000) 813–15, assumes that the population was slowly growing at an annual rate of 0.15 percent (i.e., 1 1/2 per 1,000 people), from about 45 million in 14 A.D. to a peak of about 61 million in 164, including the entry of 20,000 slaves annually from outside the frontiers. Average life expectancy and survival rates: Saller (1994) 12–25. The comments about the absorption of surplus births replicate the argument of Wrigley (1978) 218, on early modern London; Jongman (2003), develops a similar argument for the entire urban population of Italy and suggests that since "the manumission of slaves . . . probably would have made up for a large part of the natural decrease of the free urban population" (118), most of the immigrants to Rome were new slaves; in contrast, Lo Cascio (2006) 65, argues "that there are no a priori reasons . . . to believe that deaths strongly outnumbered births in Rome for the whole of antiquity." Epitaph at Hierapolis: Cagnat (1906–1927) 4:290–91, no. 841.

[13] For the boom in the production of olive oil in North Africa, see Mattingly (1988). Quotation about public policies from Garnsey (2000) 692; also Pleket (1993) 30, "Like all megalopolises Rome unintentionally stimulated economic activities elsewhere," and Morley (2007) 590, "The emperors were concerned with supplying the army and the city of Rome, not with maintaining Italian agriculture and industry."

services, but instead commandeered much of its vast imports through the imposition of taxes. In fact, in return for grain and other supplies the only commodity that provincials received from Italy in bulk was sand, used as ballast in empty ships on their return voyages. The capital paid for its supplies with dirt. Rome had become a larger version of classical Sparta, a city of special citizens sustained through the efforts of millions of provincial helots. In the early empire the presence of Rome may have stimulated the economy because of the demands imposed by its enormous size, but it remained "essentially a parasite city."[14]

Why Was Rome So Large for So Long?

The conquest of the entire Mediterranean provided emperors with the resources to support an enormous city. But simply having the capability does not answer the questions of why the early emperors decided to devote those resources to supplying Rome at this huge level, and why subsequent emperors not only sustained that concentration of resources for centuries, but even enhanced it by providing more free foodstuffs, more buildings, and more amenities. In other ancient kingdoms rulers who could accumulate considerable resources had often indulged in gigantic vanity projects and prestige monuments, such as ziggurats, pyramids, or huge burial mounds. "Monumental architecture is both a sign of power and an instrument of power." This tendency continued into the post-Roman period. During the eighth century, for instance,

---

[14] For the guild of *saburrarii*, "sand diggers," see Sirks (1991) 264–65. Quotation about parasite city from Garnsey and Saller (1987) 8, following Finley (1985) 130, "the complete parasite-city." For more benign, positive perspectives on the impact of Rome, see Hopkins (2002) 229, "the city of Rome served as the main motor of economic integration," and Erdkamp (2005) 330, emphasizing the benefits over the burdens: "Rome, far from being a parasitic city, stimulated growth by creating a stable market for all kind of goods and services." The arguments in favor of modest economic growth under the early empire assume an increase in productivity: see Hopkins (1983) xvi–xix, Saller (2002), and Hitchner (2002, 2005). In contrast, note Finley (1985) 182, preferring "the possibility of exploitation without any increase in productivity."

various medieval rulers in Europe mobilized their populations to dig large ditches in the countryside, including canals, dikes, and fences, which were "intimately bound up with the exercise of power and its justification." The symbolic meanings of these trenches far outweighed their strategic value or utilitarian functions: "the almost ritual digging of ditches . . . was a theatrical act." As their equivalent of pyramids or ditches, Roman emperors committed themselves to underwriting a huge city at vast expense and effort for centuries.[15]

This commitment to maintaining the enormity of Rome is all the more surprising because leaders in the Republic and then early emperors had already been aware of the risks. In the later Republic the initial response to the increasing size of Rome had been to move people out by giving them land in colonies, first throughout Italy, then overseas. Julius Caesar and Augustus both tried to reduce the number of recipients of grain doles. Caesar, for instance, sent 80,000 citizens to colonies outside Italy; Augustus even contemplated eliminating the grain doles entirely. Yet neither made much of a dent in the overall population of Rome. Instead, they seemed to encourage its expansion. Caesar offered Roman citizenship to doctors and teachers who were willing to live at Rome, and Augustus went on a binge of expanding and improving the city's infrastructure. Subsequent emperors likewise, rather than reducing the demands by reducing the population, instead were willing to endure and respond to complaints about shortages. In 51, people were so worried about a shortage of grain that they threw bread crusts at the emperor Claudius in the Forum. He immediately arranged for the transportation of more grain, even though it was the middle of winter. One historian was left shaking his head at this precarious situation: "the survival of the Roman people is entrusted to ships and misfortunes."[16]

---

[15] Quotation about monumental architecture from Christian (2004) 261; about medieval ditches from Squatriti (2002) 16–17.

[16] Suetonius, *Iulius* 41.3, recipients, 42.1, colonies, citizenship, *Augustus* 42.3, elimination, *Claudius* 18.2, bread crusts. Tacitus, *Annales* 12.43, winter, survival, with Garnsey (1988) 218–27, for examples of food shortages at Rome

In terms of the effort required to sustain the scale and complexity of its logistical supply for so many centuries, the size of Rome made little sense in this sort of underdeveloped, unmechanized, preindustrial agrarian economy. But in terms of articulating and projecting a particular grand narrative about Roman imperial history, it was vital. The enormous size of Rome confirmed a particular myth about emperorship, it provided a venue at which emperors could perform their emperorship, and it was a visible guarantee of security and peace for outlying provinces. Great size might be a powerful symbol. The size of Rome hence represented an ideological commitment to a particular historical narrative, a particular notion of emperorship, and a particular idea of empire.[17]

First, promoting Rome allowed emperors to sustain the claim that their rule was an extension of the Republic. The Republic had been established in the later sixth century B.C. as a replacement for and an antidote to monarchy. Its political structure had been the opposite of kingship: collegiate magistrates, rather than rule by one man; selection of magistrates by elections, rather than dynastic succession; rotation of offices, tenures of only one year, and limited possibilities of repeating offices, rather than lifetime rule. In the Republic, "kingship" became a term of abuse. As a result, even though emperorship of course appeared to have revived characteristics of monarchy, Augustus and most subsequent emperors avoided any association with kingship. Critics may have claimed that Rome in her old age under emperors resembled Rome in her infancy under kings. Emperors themselves, however, repeatedly insisted that they had truly revived the Republic.[18]

---

in the early empire. For the difficulty in sailing from Alexandria to Rome against the prevailing winds, see Rickman (1980) 129: "Egyptian grain was thus not so easily within Rome's grasp."

[17] Note Finley (1985) 159, distinguishing "the problem of feeding the populace of Rome from economic activity in general." For a general examination of the emergence of giant cities in history, see Ades and Glaeser (1995): "political forces, even more than economic factors, drive urban centralization" (195).

[18] Criticism: Lactantius, *Institutiones divinae* 7.15.14–16, "quasi ad alteram infantiam revoluta," attributed to Seneca, i.e., Seneca the Elder.

Rome functioned as part of the proof of their revival. Their care for the city and its residents demonstrated, on an enormous scale, the sincerity of their commitment to the Republic. Augustus had set the tone in his catalogue of his own achievements by listing the expenses and other burdens he had undertaken on behalf of "the Republic and the Roman people." Even though he conceded that he had in the past seized power, he claimed that he had done so in order to save the Republic and that he had restored control to "the senate and Roman people" once the civil wars were over. Most of his successors maintained this pretense of decorum and deference. Trajan in particular acquired a reputation for his respectful behavior. According to a panegyric by Pliny the Younger, Trajan had patiently attended his ceremonial election to a consulship in 100, and afterward he had recited the oath of office before the presiding magistrate: "you subordinated yourself to the laws."[19]

One important audience for the emperors' patronage of Rome was senators. In the Republic senators had dominated. They had commanded the armies that expanded the empire and had celebrated magnificent triumphs at Rome; they had governed the overseas provinces; they had displayed their wealth and prestige by funding the construction of buildings and monuments at Rome. When the king of Bithynia had visited Rome in the mid-second century B.C., he had addressed the senators as "savior gods." Under the rule of emperors, however, senators had been effectively demoted. Since they were no longer able or allowed to compete with imperial power and imperial resources, the best they could do now was serve in the imperial administration. Smart emperors nevertheless recognized the vital importance of senators by appointing them to offices in the provincial administration. They also acknowledged that senators still functioned as the guardians of Republican traditions. Trajan, for instance, was praised for acting "just like senators." As consul he had visited the

---

[19] Augustus, *Res gestae* praef., expenses, 34.1, restoration. Pliny, *Panegyricus* 63, attendance at election, oath, 65.1, laws.

senate house and offered prayers for the benefit of the Republic. During one debate he had presided, and senators could express their opinions freely. Honoring senatorial traditions at Rome was a way for emperors to show respect for the traditions of the Republic. Since the behavior of Augustus and Trajan in particular had lived up to senatorial expectations, it is not surprising that in the later empire the highest praise senators could bestow on an emperor was to proclaim him "more fortunate than Augustus, better than Trajan."[20]

Second, the emperors needed a stage to display their imperial power. The foundation of imperial rule did not consist of a constitution or a legal document ratified by the Roman state. Instead, Augustus had started out as a warlord, like his rivals, and after his victory in the civil wars he had ruled as a wealthy patron presiding over networks of supporters. Augustus had built upon that informal, personal authority to acquire official magistracies and titles. Subsequent emperors received many of the same magistracies and titles, which therefore seemed to define a formal "office" of emperor. Despite this gradual routinization of imperial office, however, every emperor had to demonstrate, over and over, his power and influence. In place of the politics of elections, they relied on public appearances and public performances. Even the successes they earned through military victories on the frontiers had to be displayed and acknowledged at Rome.

Rome hence became a huge stage set for the exhibition of emperorship. Those performances typically included grand gestures of generosity. Most of the great buildings and monuments were funded by imperial resources. Trajan, for instance, used the booty from his victory over the Dacians to build a new forum that was larger than the previous forums of Augustus, Vespasian, and Nerva combined. His forum included an expansive courtyard entered through a central arch and framed by long colonnades,

[20] King Prusias: Polybius, *Historiae* 30.18.5. Pliny, *Panegyricus* 63.6, "just like senators," 66.2, senate house, 72.1, prayers, 76.1–2, debate. Senatorial acclamation: Eutropius, *Breviarium* 8.5.3.

a large basilica that housed libraries, and another courtyard surrounded by a curved colonnade. The most impressive monument in this rear courtyard was a tall column, decorated with a spiral frieze depicting scenes from the war with the Dacians. With its many expensive marble columns and bronze statues, "the unmistakable signs of an overwhelming imperial prosperity and achievement," Trajan's forum memorialized the successes of imperial rule. It also memorialized the emperor himself. A statue of Trajan stood atop the tall column; in the center of the front courtyard was a colossal equestrian statue of the emperor. Even though subsequent emperors added decorations to the forum complex, it always remained a reminder of Trajan's greatness, a "memorial for himself."[21]

Trajan's generosity included bread and circuses. According to one historian, Trajan "knew that the Roman people were especially concerned about two interests, the supply of grain and the spectacles." He enlarged and enhanced the Circus Maximus, which had already become "a suitable venue for advertising the strength of the empire and the achievements of its rulers." To celebrate his Dacian victory he presented games at Rome that lasted for 123 days and that featured the combats of 10,000 gladiators and the slaughtering of 11,000 animals. In order to protect the grain ships he also excavated a new inner harbor at Portus, just north of the port city of Ostia at the mouth of the Tiber. After Trajan's reign, as each emperor tried to surpass the accomplishments of his predecessors, Rome acquired more and larger amenities. The Baths of Caracalla provided seating for 1600 bathers; a century later, even as the size of Rome was finally beginning to diminish, the new Baths of Diocletian could accommodate almost twice as many. In person or through statues and images, emperors

---

[21] Quotation about imperial prosperity from Packer (2001) 187; also Edwards and Woolf (2003) 12: "The City was a showpiece of imperial munificence." Memorial for himself: Dio, *Historiae Romanae* 68.16.3, with Patterson (1992) 209, on the imagery of Trajan's forum, which "combined to present the emperor as a *triumphator* in republican style."

validated the legitimacy of their imperial rule through their public displays at Rome.[22]

Third, the magnificence of Rome sent messages to provincials. One message was meant to reassure them about their own security. Provincials supported the extravagances of the capital. In return for their contributions of food, marble, and manpower, they were for the most part not reimbursed with cash or goods. Instead, they received a guarantee of peace within the empire and security on the frontiers. According to a speech put into the mouth of a Roman commander in the later first century, Roman emperors protected the Rhine frontier in order to defend the provincials of Gaul from Germans. But that protection came with a price. "Peace among tribes cannot be maintained without soldiers, soldiers cannot be maintained without wages, and wages cannot be maintained without taxes." The warranty of that security was Rome. *Pax et Urbs*: "therefore," this fictional speech concluded, "love and support peace and the city."[23]

Another message for provincials, however, was more domineering. In the past Rome had conquered these outlying regions. The immediate consequences of those losses had often been devastating: destruction of cities, plundering of artworks, even mass enslavement. The political consequences had included the imposition of provincial administration and taxation. In the long term, of course, inclusion in the Roman Empire had been beneficial for many provincials, especially the local notables who had acquired Roman citizenship, served in imperial offices, and even

[22] Grain and spectacles: Fronto, *Principia historiae* 17. Quotation about venue from Coleman (2000) 215, in an excellent survey of entertainments at Rome. Games: Dio, *Historiae Romanae* 68.15.1. Seating in baths: Olympiodorus, *Frag.* 41, with DeLaine (1997) 224, on the symbolism of baths: "the finished building was a permanent reminder of the power to command resources wielded by . . . the emperor alone."

[23] Taxes, peace, and city: Tacitus, *Historiae* 4.74, with Elton (2005), on why provincials in Cilicia and Syria would tolerate the presence of troops: "the needs of the army . . . were probably not beneficial to local economies. . . . [But] an army . . . was a vital necessity" (300).

earned senatorial rank. But the payment of taxes had remained as a mark of inferiority and subordination. Provincials paid taxes; Roman citizens in Italy did not. Rome had first claim to imperial resources throughout the empire. In the early second century an emperor politely informed the representatives of Ephesus to queue up for access to surplus grain from Egypt: "first the ruling city must have a bountiful [supply of the] grain that has been prepared for the market and collected from everywhere; then other cities likewise may acquire their supplies." As one orator noted to the emperor Trajan, Egypt was to remember that "it was offering us not just food, but tribute. Let Egypt know that . . . she serves the Roman people."[24]

The Mediterranean might hence be viewed as the puddle formed in the gigantic ecological and economic footprint of Rome. In this Mediterranean perspective the enormous size of Rome was an overwhelming representation of power. Taxation, including in particular the supply of the capital, was a form of symbolic imperialism, a constant reminder to provincials that they were the conquered and Rome was the conqueror. For the magnificent buildings at Rome, emperors facilitated the importation of colored marble from quarries all over the empire, at great expense and effort. This consumption of provincial marble emphasized "the symbolism of conquest and overseas influence." For the extravagant games at Rome, emperors imported exotic animals from all over the empire, including lions, leopards, and elephants from Africa and Asia, crocodiles, hippopotamuses, and rhinoceroses from Egypt, bulls from Thessaly, wild pigs from Germany and Gaul, and bears from Spain. These animals were emblematic proxies for their original provinces and frontier regions. Their slaughter was a reenactment, and a reminder, of past victories: imperialism overseas was transformed into entertainment at Rome. For the city's food supply, emperors imported grain, olive oil, and wine

---

[24] Ephesus: Wörrle (1971), discussing a fragment of an imperial rescript inscribed at Ephesus and identifying "the ruling city" as Rome. Egypt: Pliny, *Panegyricus* 31.3.

from overseas. In place of onetime military conquest, now Rome ate its empire, over and over. From the perspective of the residents of Rome, its Mediterranean empire looked like an enormous dinner table.[25]

As an ideological construct "Rome" was a pledge to senators that emperors still respected the traditions of the Republic, an opportunity for emperors to display their wealth and influence before large audiences, and a guarantee to the provincials of their security. "Rome" was a medium for constructing a reality in which the privileged residents of the capital took priority over the subordinated residents of the outlying provinces. Because of its incessant demands, Rome had become "a mighty beating heart, causing everything to move at its own rhythm." The larger Rome remained, the greater the effectiveness of "Rome" as an idiom of domination and subordination.[26]

New Priorities

By the later third and early fourth century, however, these ideological motives for sustaining the size of Rome had changed considerably. Not only was the idea of "Rome" losing its potency as a signifier about the survival of the Republic, the performance of emperorship, and the subservience of the provinces; the city itself was being marginalized in Roman society.

First, emperors increasingly looked to different ideologies and different institutions to justify their imperial rule. Septimius Severus may have studied at Athens before becoming emperor in the late second century. In contrast, many of his successors during the third and fourth centuries were career soldiers who

---

[25] Quotation about symbolism from Fant (1993) 148; also 160: "Italy was lavishly supplied with the major colored marbles, whereas they remained scarce in the provinces." Variety of animals: Claudian, *De consulatu Stilichonis* 3.285–369, on the animals supplied for games celebrating the consul Stilicho at Rome in 400. For the world as a dinner table, see Plutarch, *Quaestiones convivales* 7.4.7.704B.

[26] Quotation about heart from Braudel (1981) 528, describing early modern London.

had not been educated in Roman history. One of them, in fact, belittled classical culture as "slime and a public menace." These emperors were not as committed to linking their authority to the traditions of the Republic.[27]

Instead, these emperors depended much more explicitly on the support of their troops. Senators had less and less influence in the selection or even confirmation of new emperors. "The power of the army grew, and the empire and the right of selecting an emperor were snatched from the senate." During the third century, in most cases the senate at Rome recognized new emperors only after they had been proclaimed by soldiers on the frontiers. As one emperor reminded the senate, "I may disregard [your] comments, because I have weapons and soldiers." The rise of these soldier emperors seemed to confirm the advice Septimius Severus had once given his sons: "enrich the soldiers, and ignore everyone else."[28]

The loyalty of soldiers was often fickle, however, and during the third century emperors who were unsuccessful in military campaigns typically were killed. As a result, another source of imperial legitimacy was association or even identification with divine power. In the later third century the emperor Aurelian hoped to end an uprising among soldiers by insisting that they had no role in establishing or ending his rule. "He said that the soldiers were mistaken if they supposed that the destiny of emperors was in their hands. For he said that god [Jupiter] alone had bestowed the purple robe and had measured the length of a reign." The emperor Diocletian and his co-emperors in the Tetrarchy went further and effectively identified themselves with Jupiter, "the ruler of the heavens," and Hercules, "the pacifier of the earth." Constantine, even though a Christian emperor, nevertheless continued this trend of identifying with divine power. Eusebius, bishop of Caesarea in Palestine, neatly illustrated

---

[27] Licinius' attitude toward culture: *Epitome de Caesaribus* 41.8.

[28] Power of army: Aurelius Victor, *De Caesaribus* 37.5. Dio, *Historiae Romanae* 77.15.2, Septimius Severus' advice, 78.20.2, Caracalla's response to senate.

this new notion of Christian emperorship in his sequential accounts of Constantine's rise to power. When he first described Constantine's accession in 306, he noted the role of the army in the proclamation. A few years later when he described the same accession, he claimed that God had chosen Constantine before the proclamation by the army. But by the time Eusebius again described the same accession after Constantine's death in 337, he omitted any reference to the army and highlighted only God's role: "on his own God, the ruler of the entire universe, selected Constantine." In these successive accounts Eusebius had transformed Constantine from a soldier emperor characteristic of the third century into God's chosen ruler. By the end of Constantine's reign, Eusebius had essentially made the emperor into an analogue of Jesus Christ. In one panegyric he described both Constantine and the Savior as "a prefect of the Great Emperor," that is, of God. By now Eusebius and Constantine were both far from thinking about imperial rule in terms of the traditional expectations about acting like a Republican emperor.[29]

For soldier emperors, and subsequently for soldier emperors who were also Christian emperors, maintaining Rome was simply not a top priority. Instead, they supported and enlarged other institutions that competed with Rome for resources, in particular for "migrants," that is, recruits. One was the army. In the early empire maintaining a standing army of about 350,000 soldiers required about 15,000 new recruits every year. More than half of these recruits replaced soldiers who had died or been killed before completing their lengthy tenures of service, while the remainder replaced the recently discharged veterans. The army

---

[29] Aurelian's claim: Anonymus post Dionem (= Dio Continuatus), *Fragmenta* 10.6, ed. Müller (1851) 197 = [Peter the Patrician], *Fragmenta* 178. Jupiter and Hercules: *Panegyrici latini* 10(2).11.6. Constantine's accession: Eusebius, *Historia ecclesiastica* 8, Appendix 5, published in late 313 or 314; *Historia ecclesiastica* 8.13.14, published before autumn 316; *Vita Constantini* 1.24. Prefect: Eusebius, *De laudibus Constantini* 3.5, 7.13, with Van Dam (2007a) 290–92, for the date, delivered at Constantinople during the summer of 336.

was constantly exchanging older men for more than twice as many young men. These fresh recruits were similar to the 10,000 immigrants required every year to sustain the huge population of Rome, but with the important difference that the army recruited only men. As a result, even though the army was about one-third the size of Rome, it was absorbing the young men from a birth cohort that was effectively three times the size of the birth cohort producing migrants to Rome. Then Diocletian in the later third century and subsequent emperors enlarged the size of the army, perhaps by a considerable percentage, and increased its demand for new recruits by a similar percentage. Another competing institution was the church. By extending privileges to bishops and other churchmen, Constantine and subsequent Christian emperors created a "huge army of clergy and monks." A century after Constantine the total number of bishops and clerics in the empire was approximately one-third, perhaps even one-half, the size of the Roman army. The fraternity of churchmen and monks was another all-male institution that could be replenished only from outside its ranks.[30]

In the face of the demand for recruits (and resources) from the enlarged army of soldiers and the new militia of clerics and monks, the loser was the city of Rome. Recruitment into the army diverted young men toward the frontiers, while recruitment into the clergy and into monasteries encouraged young men to stay in their native provinces and hometowns. The earlier

---

[30] The size of the early imperial army is notoriously difficult to estimate: see MacMullen (1980), suggesting 350,000 soldiers in the Severan army. Scheidel (2007) 432, argues that the early imperial army required 15,000 new recruits annually, while discharging 6,000–7,000 veterans each year. Enlargement of army: Campbell (2005) 124, "the Severan army may have been at least doubled, though doubtless the real establishment rarely matched the paper strength"; Whitby (2000a) 292, suggests perhaps 435,000 soldiers under Diocletian. Quotation about army of clergy from Jones (1964) 933; also 686, "The army was a heavy drain on the limited manpower of the empire, and an even heavier incubus on its meagre economic resources." For the number of bishops and clerics, see Van Dam (2007b) 351–52.

concern of emperors to establish their respect for the Republican traditions of Rome could not compete with the new pressures on the frontiers and the new requirements of Christianity. As a result, emperors began to downgrade the status of Rome and Italy. It is not surprising that at the end of the third century Diocletian imposed taxes on northern Italy, and that his successor Galerius extended taxation to peninsular Italy and the city of Rome. Italy was now being treated like a province, and Rome like a provincial city.[31]

Second, after the third century emperors were anyway hardly visiting Rome at all. Diocletian arrived at Rome in 303 to assume a consulship and celebrate the twentieth anniversary of his accession. But when he could no longer endure the outspoken comments of the people of Rome, he did not even wait out a freezing rainstorm before leaving in haste. A few years later the emperor Galerius marched on Rome to eliminate a rival. Because he had never visited before, "he imagined that the city was not much larger than the cities he was familiar with" in the provinces. His ignorance wrecked his campaign, however, because as soon as he saw Rome, he immediately realized that he had not brought enough troops to surround the walls. During his long reign of over thirty years, Constantine visited Rome only three times, for a total stay of about five months. After his death in 337 most emperors stayed away.[32]

In 357 Constantius finally arrived at Rome twenty years after becoming emperor. Visiting Rome had obviously not been high on his list of priorities. Initially he rode into the city seemingly prepared for a military campaign, surrounded by soldiers in full

---

[31] New taxes: Lactantius, *De mortibus persecutorum* 23.1–6, 26.2; also Aurelius Victor, *De Caesaribus* 39.31, "the oppressive evil of taxes." Note that the army and the church were also recruiting against each other; see Lenski (2004), for the emperor Valens' attempts to force monks into military service: "The tug of war between a monastic and military career was thus very real in the 370s" (102–3).

[32] Lactantius, *De mortibus persecutorum* 17.1–3, Diocletian at Rome, 27.2, Galerius' invasion.

armor, "as if his battle line had been drawn up." For Constantius this was normal behavior, "as if he intended to frighten the Euphrates frontier or the Rhine frontier with a show of weapons." At Rome, however, such a military demeanor that was characteristic of the frontiers was out of place, and Constantius quickly adjusted. He toured the sights with senators as his guides, and he spoke in the senate house. In contrast to Diocletian, he even enjoyed the witty banter of the people. For a month Constantius behaved like a proper Republican emperor at Rome. Then news arrived about pillaging in the Balkans, and he immediately left for the frontier.[33]

Like other emperors of the late third and fourth centuries, Constantius spent most of his time in cities that were near the frontiers, such as Trier, Milan, Serdica (modern Sofia), Sirmium, Thessalonica, Constantinople, and Antioch. In these frontier capitals itinerant emperors now constructed the huge buildings in which they could demonstrate their imperial power. At Trier, for instance, Constantine and his sons financed the sort of buildings that were common at Rome, including a new basilica to serve as a large reception chamber, a new bath complex, repairs to the amphitheater, and an expansion of the circus. As one panegyrist reminded Constantine, "all these buildings are the gifts of your presence." As a result, emperors could perform their rulership elsewhere than at Rome. Constantius often watched the games in the circus at Antioch. Julian received soldiers in his palace at Paris, "shining in the clothing of an emperor." Another emperor, perhaps Gratian, appeared at the entertainments at Trier: "in the afternoon the emperor was captivated by the spectacles in the circus." Emperors no longer needed Rome as a stage for performing their emperorship.[34]

[33] Ammianus Marcellinus, *Res gestae* 16.10.4, battle line, 6, Euphrates, 9, "qualis in provinciis suis visebatur," 13, witty shouts, 20, departure.

[34] Buildings at Trier: *Panegyrici latini* 6(7).22.5–6, with Wightman (1970) 98–123, on imperial construction at Trier. Ammianus Marcellinus, *Res gestae*

In terms of the presence of emperors, increasingly the empire was divided in half along a diagonal line distinguishing the northern and eastern regions from the southern and western regions. After the reigns of the Tetrarchic emperors in the early fourth century, emperors no longer visited the provinces in the south, from Spain through North Africa and Egypt to Palestine. Instead, they spent almost all of their time along the great arc that extended from Trier in northern Gaul along the Rhine and Danube rivers through northern Italy and the Balkans, and then through central and eastern Asia Minor to Antioch in Syria. After the reign of Valens in the later fourth century, however, they shortened the arc to the northern sweep between Trier and Constantinople, no longer visiting the provinces in Syria or even central Asia Minor. After the abandonment of the provinces in Britain, Gaul, Spain, and North Africa to the barbarians during the fifth century, they shortened the arc even further, merely to the sweep between northern Italy and Constantinople. As the empire seemed to shrink in size, Rome was quite thoroughly marginalized. By now Rome had become a typical endangered town on the periphery of imperial interests. At the end of the sixth century the bishop of Rome was asking the emperor at Constantinople for more soldiers to defend against the Lombards: "Rome has been abandoned." The empire had been turned inside out, and Rome was now a mere frontier outpost.[35]

Third, this limitation on the presence of emperors and the effectiveness of Roman troops dramatically changed the dynamic between Rome and the provincials concerning the benefits of Roman rule. In the past, the establishment of garrisons and the stationing of troops on the frontiers had seemingly guaranteed the safety of the provinces. In the later first century the famous orator Dio Chrysostom reminded the people of Rhodes that

---

20.4.22, Julian at Paris, 21.6.3, Constantius at Antioch. Emperor in the circus: Augustine, *Confessiones* 8.6.15.

[35] Abandoned: Gregory I, *Registrum* 5.36.

under Roman rule they no longer had to worry about expenditures on their own fleet of battleships: "the moment for such concerns is gone; now you live in peace." In reality, of course, while the interior provinces were quite peaceful, the frontiers had always remained zones of interaction. Even when there were no military campaigns, there was constant movement back and forth across the frontiers. Since the frontiers typically corresponded to the ecological transition from agriculture to cattle breeding and pastoralism, the Roman army in fact acquired supplies from both sides. Those supplies increasingly included manpower, as the Roman army recruited neighboring barbarians and settled tribes on reservations inside the frontiers. By then the realities of frontier societies were challenging the old ideology that had insisted on a firm distinction between "Romans" and "barbarians." In the mid-fourth century Trier was still represented in an illustrated calendar as a muscle-bound Amazon warrior intimidating a barbarian captive. Back then those prisoners might be forced to entertain the locals by fighting wild animals in the amphitheater. But after more barbarian groups had crossed the Rhine, a century later the people of Trier were themselves taking shelter in their amphitheater. The deliberate recruitment of barbarians had mutated into hostile invasions by barbarians. Not only were Roman garrisons no longer a guarantee of security; in some frontier regions there were no more emperors, and often no more Roman troops. Now it was difficult to maintain even the hope of security.[36]

In frontier regions provincials increasingly organized their own protection, first under the leadership of local aristocrats and warlords and then with the support of local bishops and monks. On the eastern frontier Odenath, a local dynast at Palmyra during the 260s, defeated Persian forces that had recently captured

[36] Moment: Dio Chrysostom, *Orationes* 31.104. For the frontiers as zones of interaction, see Whittaker (1994) 85 = (2000) 315, "a compromise between the range of conquest and the economy of rule." Illustration in the Calendar of 354: see Salzman (1990), figure 5. Prisoners: *Panegyrici latini* 6(7).12.3, 12(9).23.3. Fortification of amphitheater at Trier: Fredegar, *Chronica* 2.60.

the emperor Valerian. Odenath assumed the title of "king of kings" and behaved like a Roman emperor; his son assumed the imperial title of Augustus. Subsequently Roman emperors spent more time at Antioch conducting campaigns against the Persian Empire. But after their departure in the later fourth century, locals again defended themselves. When Theodosiopolis, a city east of the Euphrates, was attacked by Persians in the early fifth century, the bishop himself commanded a catapult on the wall. On the Balkan frontier in the later 260s, Dexippus, a local aristocrat, organized resistance to the Heruls attacking Athens. Subsequently emperors resided in Balkan cities such as Serdica and Sirmium. During the fifth century, however, emperors and soldiers withdrew; soldiers from one garrison in Noricum even traveled to Italy in search of their last paycheck. Instead, in this region along the middle Danube, Severinus, a barefoot monk, served as a mediator among Romans, Goths, and other barbarian groups. On the Rhine frontier the troops hailed their commanders as local Gallic emperors during the 260s. Subsequently emperors often resided at Trier. But when they departed for good at the end of the fourth century, they also removed many of the troops. Thereafter the people in Gaul looked to bishops and local notables for protection. In the later fifth century, for example, one Gallic aristocrat established a military enclave at Soissons and assumed the title of "king of the Romans." Even as Rome seemed to have abandoned frontier provinces, provincials were struggling to remain Roman. In the past provincials had participated in the symbolic imperialism of the empire by exchanging their taxes for security; now they wanted real imperialism again. Instead, when the people of Britain requested assistance in the early fifth century, the emperor Honorius told them to defend themselves.[37]

---

[37] Odenath and Palmyra: Sartre (2005) 511–15, and Andrade (2009) 400–415. Bishop Eunomius of Theodosiopolis: Theodoret, *Historia ecclesiastica* 5.37.5–10. Dexippus at Athens: Millar (1969) 24–29, "The Roman army does not appear" (25). Garrison in Noricum: Eugippius, *Vita Severini* 20.1. Gallic empire of the third century: Drinkwater (1987). Syagrius, king of the Romans:

In late antiquity the frontiers were increasingly under more pressure from the arrival of new peoples, and emperors hence spent more time in frontier cities than at Rome. In their absence the supply of grain to the capital might sometimes break down, and there was even the chance that a resident of Rome might have to watch the spectacles in the Circus Maximus on an empty stomach. Emperors furthermore justified their rule in terms of divine legitimation, and they were concerned about the loyalty of their soldiers. But when they could no longer keep garrisons on the frontiers, they withdrew. Contraction of the frontiers, neglect of the capital, disregard of the traditions of the Republic: contemporary historians could sense that the trajectory of Roman history had gone off track.[38]

New Histories for an Old Capital

When Aurelius Victor composed an epitome of Roman imperial history in the mid-fourth century, one of his recurring themes was the celebration of the centennial anniversaries of the foundation of the city of Rome. In his survey he carefully noted that the emperor Claudius had "wondrously" presided over the 800th anniversary of the foundation, that Antoninus Pius had "magnificently" celebrated the 900th anniversary, and that Philip the Arab had commemorated the millennium anniversary in 248 "with games of all sorts." These millennial games had displayed a fantastic bestiary collected from around the empire, including sixty lions, thirty-two elephants, thirty leopards, ten tigers, ten elks, ten giraffes, six hippopotamuses, and one rhinoceros, as well as one thousand pairs of gladiators. A century later, however, when the festivities in honor of the 1100th anniversary should

---

Van Dam (2005) 196. Honorius' letter: Zosimus, *Historia nova* 6.10.2, with Whitby (2000b) 480–85, on the "remilitarization of local society."

[38] For the possibility of hunger at the Circus, see Prudentius, *Contra Symmachum* 2.948, "quis venit esuriens magni ad spectacula circi?"; with Tengström (1974) 47–48, on Symmachus' anxieties over the grain supply during his year as prefect of Rome.

have been celebrated, nothing had happened. Even though the emperor Constans had been in northern Italy at the time, he did not visit Rome for the anniversary. Aurelius Victor was left to mourn over this slight: "to such an extent has concern for the city of Rome dwindled day by day."[39]

Neglect of Rome had no place in the master narrative of Roman history. Earlier histories of Rome had never imagined the possibility that the capital might decline or be overlooked by emperors. At chariot races in the Circus Maximus the crowds would acclaim Rome as "immortal." Even Christian theologians were inclined to equate its supremacy with the postponement of the end times: "there seems to be no need for apprehension as long as the city of Rome survives." In the face of its disturbing abandonment, however, during the fourth century historians, senators, and churchmen began to rethink the meaning of Rome. Some of these new histories highlighted the past, presumably with the hope of reviving a lost grandeur. Some emphasized the realities of the present, as the priorities of the frontier zones dominated any nostalgia for the old capital. And still other histories looked to the future by imagining a new role for Rome as a Christian capital.[40]

One approach was an attempt to reinstate the past significance of Rome and its resident senators. As a contemporary of Aurelius Victor, Eutropius composed a summary of Roman history from the foundation of Rome to the present time at the request of the emperor Valens. Since Valens had been a career soldier and had no education at all in Roman history, Eutropius' short overview was meant to inform the emperor about the empire he was now ruling. And since Valens never visited Rome, he could also learn about the original capital of his empire.

---

[39] Aurelius Victor, *De Caesaribus* 4.14, Claudius, 15.4, Antoninus Pius, 28.1, Philip the Arab, 28.2, dwindling concern. List of animals: *Historia Augusta, Gordiani tres* 33.1–2.

[40] Immortal: Dio, *Historiae Romanae* 75.4.5. Apprehension: Lactantius, *Institutiones divinae* 7.25.6, with the discussion of Nicholson (1999).

One of Eutropius' important themes was the relentless expansion of the empire, in particular under the early emperors. Augustus had added many territories to the empire; and after subsequent emperors had merely defended rather than multiplied those provinces, "Trajan had extended the frontiers of the Roman empire far and wide." In contrast, Eutropius was critical of any abandonment of territory, in particular during his own lifetime. The recent treaty of the emperor Jovian with the Persians, in which he had surrendered some cities, was especially shameful: "this had never happened before, for almost 1,018 years since the foundation of the Roman empire." A second significant theme was the importance of the senate. According to Eutropius' account, the senate was as old as the city itself, because immediately after founding Rome the legendary king Romulus had chosen one hundred elderly men and called them senators. Once Eutropius began discussing emperors, he stressed their relations with the senate. Bad emperors treated senators badly, while good emperors treated them fairly. Trajan, for instance, never mistreated a senator, and Marcus Aurelius auctioned off his own property rather than imposing a tax on senators. Not surprisingly, Eutropius noted that these good emperors who had expanded the empire and respected the senate were still cited as models for the emperors of his day. Julian, at whose court he had himself served, was hence similar to Marcus Aurelius. According to Eutropius, emperors were to move the frontiers forward and honor the senate at Rome.[41]

Eutropius derived much of his information about the early kings of Rome and the Republic from an epitome of Livy's huge history of Rome, which had covered the period from the foundation of the city through the monarchy and Republic to the reign of Augustus. Even though Livy had been a personal friend of the first

---

[41] Eutropius, *Breviarium* 1.2.1, senators, 8.2.2, Trajan's frontiers, 8.4, Trajan and senators, 8.13, Marcus Aurelius, 10.16.3, Julian, 10.17.2, Jovian, with Bird (1993) xxvi, on how Eutropius' narrative "intended to persuade an emperor . . . of the role of the senate in Rome's history."

emperor, "it is doubtful that he believed Augustus to be the last and greatest in a long line of great men of the Republic." Instead, in his historical narrative he had seemed to prefer the Republic and its heroes to the rise of imperial rule. During the fourth century Livy was one of the classic Latin authors read by educated men at Rome, including notable senators such as Symmachus. These senators could perhaps sense that Livy's history was still directly relevant to their current situation. In the absence of emperors, senators had assumed more responsibilities for the administration of Rome, and they could almost imagine that they were living again in the Republic described by Livy. Livy's history of the Republic, when senators had dominated and there had been no emperors, seemed to match the current situation at Rome during late antiquity.[42]

During his tenure as prefect of Rome in 384, Symmachus consistently used examples from the Republic in his dispatches to the emperors who were residing in northern Italy. In a plea for the restoration of "the standing of the religions that had long benefited the Republic," he conjured up Roma, the deified personification of Rome, to address the emperors. This Roma reminded the emperors that in the past the observation of traditional religious ceremonies had saved the city's walls from invaders such as the Carthaginian general Hannibal. Even though the emperors were now Christians, Symmachus hoped to influence their decisions about religious practices by citing examples from the sacred books of Livy's history of early Rome. He also reminded emperors about their obligations to look after the people of Rome. In another dispatch he politely suggested that the emperors could satisfy the people of Rome by providing subsidies for the food supply and entertainments in the Circus Maximus. This suggestion was furthermore a tacit invitation for an emperor to visit Rome and preside in person at these games. Symmachus was hoping that the emperors would again behave like traditional Republican emperors, committed to maintaining

[42] Quotation about Livy from Luce (1990) 128. For Eutropius' sources, see Bird (1993) xliv–xlix.

the supply of Rome and receptive to the applause of the senate and people of Rome. In his perspective, only their respect for the traditions and prerogatives of Rome would ensure the integrity of the frontiers.[43]

In contrast to this sort of wishful thinking, another approach to the idea of Rome was a realistic assessment of its current marginality, an acknowledgment of its increasing insignificance in comparison to the importance of military campaigns on the frontiers. Such a history required a completely different outlook. Ammianus Marcellinus was a learned Greek from an eastern province, most likely Syria or Phoenicia, and a professional soldier. As "a soldier and a Greek," which we might translate as "an officer and a gentleman," he was quite the opposite of the senators at Rome. Ammianus visited the capital probably during the early 380s. In his historical narrative, however, he seemed to imply that Rome was no longer worth supporting. Ammianus mocked the pretensions of the senators at Rome. He claimed that they were not as learned as they pretended, since their "libraries were shut up forever in the manner of tombs," and he noted that they certainly were not military men. Their version of a military campaign was a leisurely convoy to their country estates, which they considered "the equivalent of the campaigns of Caesar." He likewise mocked the behavior of ordinary people at Rome, including their sense of entitlement about the supply of wine and their obsession with chariot races: "their temple . . . is the Circus Maximus." Because he seemed to have no particular regard for the senate or for the special prerogatives of the people of the capital, Ammianus was clearly not about to buy into the bargain of maintaining Rome at the expense of provincials like himself. His conclusion about affairs at Rome was an intellectual justification for both his own

---

[43] Symmachus, *Relationes* 3.3, standing of religions, 3.9, Roma, 6, subsidies and entertainments, 9.8, senate and people, with Lim (1999), on the secularization of the games at Rome, and Chenault (2008), on the senate at Rome during the fourth century. Symmachus once promised to send a complete edition of Livy to a friend: see Symmachus, *Epistulae* 9.13.

and the emperors' absence from the capital: "nothing memorable or worthwhile is done at Rome." Like the emperors, Ammianus spent most of his professional military career instead on the northern and eastern frontiers.[44]

Another alternative likewise started with a recognition of the insignificance of Republican traditions, but this time in comparison to the rising prominence of Christianity. Emperors had begun to offer their support and patronage to Christianity only since the reign of Constantine. As a result, bishops had soon started to promote their own privileges and influence. Symmachus' dispatches had been sent to the court of Valentinian II in Milan. There his plea for the restoration of traditional religious practices ran into opposition from the city's bishop. Ambrose was a member of a distinguished senatorial family who had himself once initiated a career in the imperial administration. But now, as a bishop he was not prepared to show the same reverence for the traditions of the Republic. Instead, he tried to convince Valentinian to reject Symmachus' request in two letters, one composed before he had even seen the original petition, the second a detailed refutation. In this refutation he mocked the prefect's arguments. In his estimation, Symmachus' evocation of the goddess Roma had been pointless, since in fact Hannibal and other enemies had been able to threaten and nearly topple the Roman state. Instead, Ambrose cited examples from Roman history of the ineffectiveness of the cults and traditions of Rome. In both of his letters he furthermore addressed Valentinian II as "Christian emperor," even "most Christian emperor." These titles implicitly defined a new perspective on imperial rule. Not only should Christian emperors no longer support traditional cults and priesthoods. In addition, in these "Christian times" bishops alone should have the prerogative to judge religious matters. Ambrose's argument about the deference of Christian emperors was simultaneously an argument

---

[44] Ammianus Marcellinus, *Res gestae* 14.6.1, not learned, wine, 18, tombs, 25, chariot races, 26, nothing memorable, 28.4.18, campaigns of Caesar, 29, Circus Maximus, 31.16.9, "miles quondam et Graecus."

about the promotion of bishops. He apparently assumed that this argument could be especially convincing for an emperor who was not at Rome, surrounded by all the reminders of an old-style, pre-Christian, Republican emperorship.[45]

Ambrose noted that the opposition to an earlier attempt to restore these traditional cults had been led by Damasus, the bishop of Rome. Damasus had also been active in highlighting the prominence of churches and shrines at the capital. The early churches had been built away from the center of Rome, either just inside the walls or in the suburbs. Constantine himself had initiated construction of the Church of St. John Lateran, at the southeastern edge of the city inside the walls; his mother was buried in a mausoleum attached to the Church of St. Marcellinus and St. Peter, in an eastern suburb; his daughters were buried in a mausoleum next to the Church of St. Agnes, in a northern suburb. The Church of St. Peter, also initiated probably by Constantine, was in a western suburb, across the Tiber River, on a hill that was not one of the original seven. For Christians the suburban hinterland was more important than the old city center and its lofty buildings. Now the old monuments, both secular and religious, were being ignored. According to one part-time resident, "the golden sheen of the Capitoline Hill is filthy, and all the temples of Rome are covered with soot and cobwebs. The city is being moved from its foundations. The people rush past the ruins of the temples and hurry to the martyrs' tombs." The leading impresario of these catacombs was Damasus, who composed the verse epigrams inscribed in the shrines honoring the martyrs. This new Christian Rome, at least initially, was an inverse of earlier imperial Rome twice over, both suburban and subterranean. If pagan senators were still posing as the guardians of Rome's Republican traditions, then the martyrs were now the guarantors of Rome's growing Christian reputation.[46]

---

[45] Ambrose, *Epistulae* 72.10, Christian times, 73.4–6, Roma, 7, failed cults, 10, Christian emperor.

[46] Damasus' opposition: Ambrose, *Epistulae* 72.10, with Curran (2000)

During the fourth century the new historical perspectives on Rome could take different forms. Eutropius wanted to remind emperors who never visited the old capital of the importance of the senate at Rome, while Symmachus, a leading senator at Rome, tried to influence imperial decisions by citing examples from the Republic. In contrast, Ammianus acknowledged the priority of military campaigns on the frontiers, while churchmen were reshaping the meaning of Rome in terms of Christian traditions. The increasing importance of Christianity represented the future. Subsequent emperors still did not visit Rome often. But when they did, as "Christian emperors" they conceded the significance of this new Christian topography by adjusting their performance of imperial authority.

Rome, its monuments, and its historical traditions had been constructed for the performance of Republican emperorship, not Christian emperorship. Christian emperors could hence easily offend traditional expectations. During one of his visits the emperor Constantine had declined to participate in an "ancestral festival" on the Capitoline Hill, the religious center of the city. His refusal had deeply upset the senate and the people of Rome. As a result, to become a stage for the performance of Christian emperorship Rome would have to be turned inside out, by downplaying the old center and spotlighting the ecclesiastical hinterland. In 403 the emperor Honorius visited Rome to celebrate a triumph and subsequently to assume a consulship for the next year. Before performing these traditional ceremonies, however, he first visited the Church of St. Peter to pay his respects. There "he removed his diadem and beat his breast [at the tomb] where the body of the fisherman is buried." In 500 King Theoderic of the Ostrogoths arrived at Rome. Even though he was posing as a new Roman emperor, he too first visited the Church of St. Peter "outside the city." Only then did he perform the traditional

---

142–55, "a unified Christian hinterland around the city" (148), and the excellent discussion of Damasus' role in rewriting the history of Rome in Trout (2003). Golden sheen: Jerome, *Epistulae* 107.1, with Van Dam (2007a) 131–33.

imperial duties, such as visiting the senate house, addressing the people in the city center, entering the palace in triumph, celebrating games in the Circus Maximus, and providing grain. The performance of Christian rulership at Rome, first by emperors and subsequently by barbarian kings, now gave precedence to the churches and shrines on the margins of the city. As in the empire, where the frontiers took priority over Italy and the capital at the center, so at Rome itself the Christian suburbs assumed priority over the Republican and early imperial downtown.[47]

Thinking with Rome

In the early Roman Empire, Rome was already a very ancient city. In his historical narrative Livy had located the date of its foundation by Romulus in the middle of the eighth century B.C. The Roman Empire, however, was nowhere near as old as Rome itself. Early Rome had long been dominated by its neighbors, before it had finally expanded its hegemony over central and southern Italy. Eventually Roman armies had begun to expand outside Italy, first into the western Mediterranean in campaigns against the rival empire of Carthage, then into the eastern Mediterranean in campaigns against Greek kingdoms. Rome had acquired its first overseas province, Sicily, only in the mid-third century B.C. The appearance of emperors had been even more recent, with the rise of Augustus in the later first century B.C.

City and empire had nevertheless been identified very quickly. During the fourth century one historian claimed that Romulus had been the founder of both Rome and the Roman Empire. As a result, because in their imaginations the destiny of the city seemed to have become an anticipation of the destiny of the empire, the historians of antiquity could already use Rome, or the idea of Rome, as a way to think about the empire. After the Visigoths

---

[47] Constantine: Zosimus, *Historia nova* 2.29.5. Honorius: Augustine, *Sermones Mayence* 61 = *Sermones Dolbeau* 25.26, ed. Dolbeau (1996) 266. Theoderic at Rome: *Excerpta Valesiana*, Pars posterior 12.65–67, with Arnold (2008), on the Ostrogoths in Italy.

sacked Rome in 410, for instance, one churchman immediately worried about an apocalyptic endgame: "the entire world has perished in one city." This ancient association of Rome and empire has likewise had important implications for modern historical interpretations. Modern historians too use Rome in order to think about the trajectories of the Roman Empire and the dynamics of the Mediterranean.[48]

One implication highlights the likelihood of a Mediterranean unified as a political state and integrated as an economic zone. The Roman Empire is the only state ever to have formal control over all of the Mediterranean. The empire sustained this political control over the entire coastline for well over four hundred years, between the annexation of Egypt in the later first century B.C. and the establishment of barbarian kingdoms in western provinces during the fifth century A.D. This political unification can then be taken to imply economic integration, for which the supply and maintenance of an enormous capital seem to have been confirmation. Both Rome and its empire can appear to have been the logical outcomes of a Mediterranean with an inherently natural political and economic unity.

In fact, the enormous size of Rome was completely artificial, representing the imposition of political ideology rather than a consequence of any natural ecological or economic unity in the Mediterranean. The supply of Rome represented centuries of tribute exaction, even when softened by an ideology of the benefits of Roman rule. Roman imperialism had created the means and the opportunity, and tribute exaction and redistribution, the focusing of so many resources on the enhancement of a single city, had created economic integration. The economic integration of the Mediterranean was a consequence of a political commitment to sustaining a giant capital, not a precondition for its natural emergence. As the goddess Roma, the deified personification of the

[48] Romulus: Eutropius, *Breviarium* 10.1–2. Entire world: Jerome, *Commentariorum in Ezechielem prophetam* 1, prologus (*Patrologia Latina* 25.16), with Rebenich (2009), on Jerome's reactions to barbarian invasions.

capital, once proclaimed in the later fourth century, Rome could not exist without the grain of Africa: "my enormous size is itself a burden." Without an abiding commitment to sustaining the demands of Rome, economic integration in the Mediterranean would deteriorate. And in fact, once emperors backed away from that commitment, it did disintegrate: "the spadework to foster interregional economic integration beyond the feeding of the capital barely existed."[49]

Modern historians of late antiquity hence often end up explaining the wrong end of the Roman Empire. The demise of the empire cannot be understood without first thinking about its foundation. Rather than obsessing about the downfall of the empire, we should concentrate on the motives for its initial establishment and its subsequent maintenance. The Mediterranean had never been destined to become the core of a single empire. Our starting point should not be the assumption of a centralized, unified Mediterranean, as if its subsequent fragmentation required explanation. Instead, it is the enforced integration of the Mediterranean, in favor of sustaining Rome even in the face of an underdeveloped economy and the impediments of great distance, that requires explanation. The ancient Mediterranean was unified primarily around the supply of Rome, and the maintenance of Rome as a giant capital was the consequence of an ideological decision, not an economic system. Economic stimulus and economic integration were incidental byproducts of the size of Rome; its true significance was as an ideological symbol of power and priority.

---

[49] Roma's complaint: Claudian, *De bello Gildonico* 1.108, "ipsa nocet moles." Quotation about spadework from McCormick (2001) 117; also Rickman (1980) 210, "Perhaps we have come too easily . . . to assume that because by the end of the Republic the resources of the whole Mediterranean were at Rome's call there was bound to be a successful large urban unit at the centre of it all"; Wickham (2005) 717, "it must have ultimately been the fiscal movement of goods that tied the regions together under the empire"; and Bang (2008) 294, "the economic integration created by the formation of empire in the Mediterranean happened as a consequence of tribute extraction."

A second implication focuses on our modern narratives of the transformation of the later Roman Empire. "Decline and Fall" is still a paradigm that retains its attractiveness among modern historians of late antiquity. As homage to Edward Gibbon, a charter member of the historians' hall of fame, the phrase deserves immortality. But as an interpretive scheme, it is deeply problematic. One of those concerns goes back to its original invention. In the autobiographical memoirs that he was still writing up to his death in 1794, Gibbon referred to himself as "the historian of the Decline and Fall." But he went on to point out that initially he had planned to write about "the decay of the City, rather than of the Empire." His famous retrospective description of the origin of his ideas about "Decline and Fall" reinforced this mingling in his mind between Rome and its empire. "In my Journal the place and moment of conception are recorded: the fifteenth of October 1764, in the close of evening, as I sat musing in the Church of the Zoccolanti or Franciscan friars, while they were singing Vespers in the Temple of Jupiter on the ruins of the Capitol." Gibbon had imagined the collapse of the empire by viewing the wreckage in Rome.[50]

"Decline and Fall" is a fundamentally inadequate way of imagining the transition of the Roman Empire: too abrupt, too teleological, too moralizing, too dismissive of successor states as somehow inferior for being barbarian not Roman, Byzantine not classical, or Islamic not Christian. Gibbon had in fact already concluded *The History of the Decline and Fall of the Roman Empire* with an earlier version of his story of its origins. "It was among

---

[50] For defense of the usefulness of "decline and fall," see Liebeschuetz (2001) and Ward-Perkins (2005). Quotations from Gibbon (1984) 143, with the discussion of the variant versions in Gibbon (1966) 304–5. For the connections between Gibbon's earlier analytic studies of the topography and monuments of Rome and his later narrative history of the empire, see the comprehensive discussion in Ghosh (1997) 279–97: "The 'History of the City' was not so much abandoned as incorporated into the new work: like a Roman ruin itself, it supplied the substructure to Gibbon's intellectual triumph" (292).

the ruins of the Capitol that I first conceived the idea of a work which . . . I finally deliver to the curiosity and candour of the public." According to Gibbon, the initial inspiration of his historical narrative had also become its conclusion: the ruins of Rome. The destruction of both the city of Rome and the empire had been somehow connected to "the triumph of barbarism and religion," that is, the invasions of barbarians and the rise of Christianity. By using the city of Rome as his template for the fate of the empire, Gibbon had almost no choice but to write a historical narrative that went downhill. If only Gibbon had in addition considered the fates of other cities in the empire. Thinking about a different "Rome" might have given him, and us, a different perspective on late antiquity.[51]

---

[51] Gibbon (1932) 3:865, barbarism and religion, applied to "the ruin of ancient Rome," 880, last sentence, completed in June 1787.

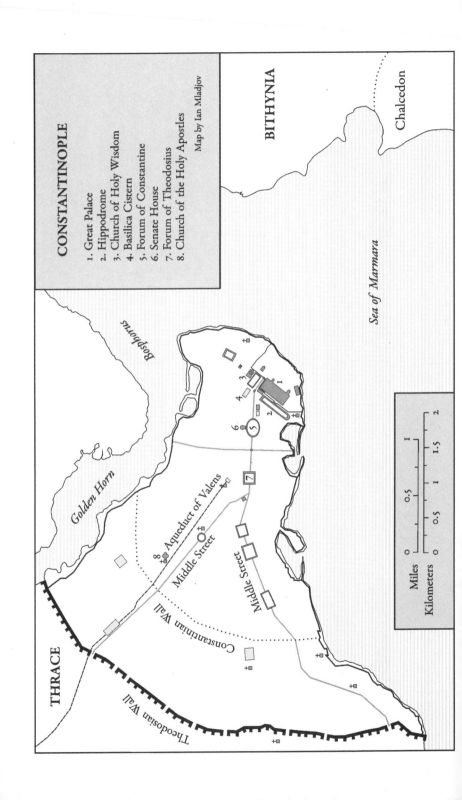

CONSTANTINOPLE

1. Great Palace
2. Hippodrome
3. Church of Holy Wisdom
4. Basilica Cistern
5. Forum of Constantine
6. Senate House
7. Forum of Theodosius
8. Church of the Holy Apostles

Map by Ian Mladjov

THRACE

BITHYNIA

Chalcedon

Sea of Marmara

Bosphorus

Golden Horn

Aqueduct of Valens

Middle Street

Middle Street

Constantinian Wall

Theodosian Wall

Miles
Kilometers

2

New Rome

In late antiquity Rome was a capital in transition. Even as its residents were under siege from barbarians such as the Visigoths, who sacked the city in 410, and the Vandals, who occupied it in 455, they were trying to cope with the loss of its supply system and hence the deterioration of many of its amenities. Now the goddess Roma, the personification of the city, was imagined to have gray hair and to be carrying a rusty spear. Not only was the capital in decline and seemingly on the verge of falling; even worse, it was being replaced, both in people's imaginations and literally. Now Rome was being characterized as "old."[1]

Other cities in which emperors had spent more time could instead be imagined to have become "Rome." According to a third-century historian, "Rome is wherever the emperor is." Most of these rival residences were on or near the northern frontiers. Diocletian had sponsored huge construction projects in order

---

[1] Roma: Claudian, *De bello Gildonico* 1.24–25. "Older Rome": Sozomen, *Historia ecclesiastica* 2.3.4; also Ammianus Marcellinus, *Res gestae* 14.6.4, "iamque vergens in senium."

to transform Nicomedia into "the equal of Rome." Constantine referred to Serdica, in the Balkans near the Danube frontier, as "my Rome." A poet described Arles, in southern Gaul, as "little Gallic Rome." Even though Arles was a Mediterranean city at the mouth of the Rhone River, it was characterized as a port supplying Trier on the Rhine frontier. Arles functioned as the equivalent of Ostia, "the mouths," for an imperial appetite now resident in northern Europe. Not surprisingly, one epitaph referred to Trier as "Belgian Rome."[2]

The most consequential of these replacement capitals was, of course, Constantinople, located between the northern frontier in the Balkans and the eastern frontier facing the Persian Empire. Inaugurated by Constantine in 330 on the site of the ancient city of Byzantium, initially the new capital might be known as Second Rome. Constantinople also acquired the *ius Italicum*, the highly prized "Italian right" that classified the city as a shareholder in the privileges of Italy. As a result, as an "Italian" city Constantinople was deemed worthy to acquire the prerogatives of "Old Rome." Both Italy and Rome had changed addresses. In contrast to "Old Rome," which seemed to be fading in obsolescence, now the most important capital was Constantinople, known as "New Rome," "Young Rome."[3]

The fates of Rome and Constantinople seemed to be heading in contrasting directions. In late antiquity Rome was still a vast outdoor museum of impressive buildings, monuments, sculptures, and dedications that commemorated the successes of its generals and emperors. Civic pride claimed that the monuments in

---

[2] Rome and emperor: Herodian, *Historiae* 1.6.5. Nicomedia: Lactantius, *De mortibus persecutorum* 7.10, with Foss (1995). Serdica: Anonymus post Dionem (= Dio Continuatus), *Fragmenta* 15.1, ed. Müller (1851) 199. Arles as Rome: Ausonius, *Ordo urbium nobilium* 10.2; as port for Trier: *Expositio totius mundi et gentium* 58. For the epitaph mentioning Trier, see Vollmer and Rubenbauer (1926).

[3] *Ius Italicum*: *Codex Theodosianus* 14.13.1, on the restoration of this rank in the early 370s. Prerogatives: *Codex Iustinianus* 11.21. "Young Rome": Sozomen, *Historia ecclesiastica* 2.3.5.

Rome had surpassed the legendary Seven Wonders of the ancient world and that the number of statues had equaled the number of residents. This gigantic accumulation of monuments was such an indiscriminate blur that the magistrate responsible for protecting all the bronze and marble statues was known simply as "the tribune in charge of the shiny stuff." Then all the shiny stuff started falling apart . . . literally. Earthquakes and fires, barbarian attacks, despoliation of marble blocks and decorative columns for use in other buildings, such as churches: now people had proof that Rome was sagging into decrepitude. Like the rotund belly of a bronze statue of an elephant in the Forum that needed to be propped up, its extravagant lifestyle had disintegrated.[4]

The standing of Rome seems to have hit bottom when eventually even a barbarian king might present himself as a Roman emperor in Italy. But when Theoderic, king of the Ostrogoths, visited Rome in 500, he found the public treasury bankrupt, filled with "nothing but hay." Now there were no more overseas provinces paying taxes, supplying exotic animals, and sending supplies of grain. Instead, the stockyards and the granaries at Rome were empty, and during one siege the people were reduced to eating the weeds growing in the ruins of the walls. Without the buttresses of taxes and subsidized food, the city's population was in free fall. At the beginning of the fifth century Rome may still have had 500,000 residents; in the middle of the fifth century its population was down to perhaps 350,000 residents; by the early sixth century it had fallen to perhaps 60,000 residents. In just over two centuries Rome had lost almost 95 percent of its population from its peak of one million residents. In contrast, more graveyards now appeared inside the walls of the city on prime real estate in the vicinity of the Colosseum, some of the imperial

---

[4] Cassiodorus, *Variae* 7.15.3, statues and residents, 4–5, Seven Wonders, 10.30.1, bronze elephants on the Via Sacra: "your foresight should reinforce [each] sagging stomach by building a wall underneath." "Tribunus rerum nitentium": *Notitia Dignitatum in partibus Occidentis* 4.17, with Ward-Perkins (1984) 38–48, on the decay of buildings at Rome already from the early fourth century.

Baths, and various churches. The old capital had become, quite accurately, a ghost town.[5]

The Ostrogoths eventually wore out their welcome in Italy, and in 537 they too besieged Rome. During one attack the soldiers at Rome resorted to wondrous ingenuity. They smashed the large marble statues of men and horses decorating the Mausoleum of Hadrian and dropped the pieces on the Goths attempting to climb the walls. In this battle the people of Rome were literally defending themselves with their own heritage. Equally as important was the assistance of their allies, the troops sent from Constantinople to drive the Goths out of Italy. Now the roles had been completely reversed, and Constantinople was trying to protect Italy and Rome. Now troops from a new capital on an old frontier were trying to save the old capital in what had become a new frontier zone.[6]

Too Much History, Not Enough History

Byzantium was not an obvious site for the foundation of a new capital. On a map it looks to be a natural gateway between Europe and Asia, and between the Black Sea and the Aegean Sea. Surrounded by water on three sides, it also appears to have been very defensible, "similar to an acropolis." In fact, it was an

---

[5] Treasury: *Anonymus Valesianus*, pars posterior 60. Procopius, *Bella* 5.23.13–23, empty stockyard (*Vivarium*) at Rome, 7.17.13, weeds; according to *Bella* 7.20.19–20, during another siege only five hundred people were left in Rome, the others having fled or died from starvation. For the estimates of the declining population cited here, see Durliat (1990) 110–25; for other estimates, see Christie (2000) 312, between 750,000 and one million residents during the fourth century; Morrisson and Sodini (2002) 172, 600,000–700,000 residents in the early fourth century, 200,000 in the early fifth century, 100,000 in ca. 500, 25,000–30,000 during the seventh century; and Christie (2006) 61, 500,000 residents in the mid-fifth century, 250,000 at the end of the fifth century, 50,000 in 600; also Wickham (2005) 34, "Demographic decline in the city of Rome was indeed probably the most important structural change in Italy between 400 and 535." For graveyards inside Rome from the fifth and sixth centuries, see Christie (2006) 252–53.

[6] Procopius, *Bella* 5.22.14, statues, 22, attack.

awkward site. On its west side it was quite vulnerable to invaders from the Balkans. Because of the prevailing winds, it was difficult to supply by sea with resources from the south, that is, from the rest of the eastern Roman Empire. Unlike Rome, it lacked an adequate source of fresh water from springs or a river. In Greek lore the ancient settlers at Chalcedon were known as "The Blind" for having overlooked the more magnificent site of Byzantium on the opposite side of the Bosphorus. In fact, perhaps they had already recognized the inadequacies of the site. Neither its geography nor its topography would seem to indicate that Byzantium was destined to become another giant capital.[7]

Nor did its past history. Before becoming Constantinople, Byzantium had been a nondescript town that had had little impact in Greek, Roman, biblical, or Christian history. In the Greek world Byzantium had been a way station for the ships that carried grain from the regions around the Black Sea through the Bosphorus and the Hellespont to Greek cities around the Aegean Sea. In the mid-fourth century B.C., for instance, King Philip of Macedonia (the father of Alexander the Great) hoped to cripple Athens by seizing Byzantium and cutting off the supply of imported grain. In the Roman world Byzantium might serve as a garrison during civil wars between emperors. In 193 the emperor Septimius Severus found his way from Thrace into Asia Minor blocked by the loss of Byzantium to a rival. He finally captured the city after an extended siege. In 324 Byzantium again became a shelter for the emperor Licinius, before he was defeated by Constantine. In the early Christian world Byzantium had no reputation. Most notably, Byzantium had not been mentioned in the books included in the New Testament. The apostle Paul had not visited, even though he had visited the vicinity of ancient Troy

---

[7] Eunapius, *Vitae sophistarum* 462, need for a south wind; Procopius, *Aedificia* 4.8.2, Byzantium as an acropolis, 5.1.8–12, winds, with Mango (1995a), for the deficiencies of the site. "The Blind" of Chalcedon: Dagron (1974) 30–31, on the disadvantages of the site of Chalcedon, but also Malkin and Shmueli (1988), on the advantages of Chalcedon for sailing patterns.

in northwestern Asia Minor. As the site of the legendary Trojan War, Troy was also famous as the home city of Aeneas, a founder of Rome whom Augustus had claimed as an ancestor. Rome was "Second Troy." In the early fourth century Constantine was thought to have considered founding his eastern capital at Troy, before settling on Byzantium. Constantinople was hence to become "Third Troy." But Paul had not previewed the significance of the site by crossing from Troy to northern Greece by way of Byzantium. Instead, he had bypassed the city by sailing to Neapolis, the port for Philippi. Byzantium had no past to speak of, Greek, Roman, biblical, or Christian.[8]

Becoming an imperial capital was therefore not an easy process for Constantinople. As a new capital it needed both basic resources and more extensive amenities. It also needed a longer, more elaborate history. During late antiquity the master narrative of the history of Rome had required revision, because it was no longer in sync with current circumstances. During the same period, the master narrative of the history of Constantinople equally required revision. This time the concern was not the outcome; it was the backstory. The problem with Rome was that it had too much history that was now incompatible with the reality of barbarian invasions and the establishment of alternative imperial residences. The problem with Constantinople, however, was that it had no history. Emperors and historians hence had to construct a new past for the new capital. Even imaginary histories would be better than no history.

---

[8] Philip and Byzantium: Demosthenes, *De corona* 87. Septimius Severus and Byzantium: Dio, *Historiae Romanae* 75.10–14, and Herodian, *Historiae* 3.1–2. Licinius: Zosimus, *Historia nova* 2.23–25. Paul at Troas: Acts of the Apostles 16:8, 11, 20:5-6, 2 Corinthians 2:12, 2 Timothy 4:13. Constantine and Troy: Sozomen, *Historia ecclesiastica* 2.3.2, and Zosimus, *Historia nova* 2.30.1. Note that Constantine claimed as an ancestor the emperor Claudius Gothicus, who in turn was thought to be descended from a Trojan king: see *Historia Augusta, Claudius* 11.9, with Van Dam (2007a) 98–100.

Christian Emperorship and an Eastern Empire

To become an imperial capital Constantinople first of all needed people. Its population grew at a volatile rate. At its inauguration in 330 it had perhaps 30,000 residents; at the beginning of the fifth century, less than a century later, its population had increased tenfold to perhaps 300,000 residents and was soon to equal the population of Rome, which was headed in the opposite direction. By the sixth century the population of Constantinople had perhaps doubled again to 600,000 residents and was ten times the size of Rome. The new capital had become "an ocean of people," which welcomed immigrants "flowing from everywhere like rivers." Most of these new residents came from the eastern provinces, in particular from Asia Minor. Some provincial cities lost so many men that they were left as "widows." In order to provide for both the increase in population and the replacements needed to sustain this high level, during the two centuries after its inauguration well over a million people moved to the new capital. This was by far the largest migration of population within the eastern Roman Empire, and the number involved far surpassed the number of barbarians who migrated into the western Roman Empire during the same period. Rome and Italy were invaded by barbarians from beyond the frontiers; Constantinople was invaded by Greeks from the provinces.[9]

[9] Population numbers from Durliat (1990) 250–57, 269; with Dagron (1974) 524–25, 530, suggesting between 200,000 and 300,000 inhabitants in the early fifth century, and Jones (1964) 698, endorsing the high number for the sixth century. In contrast, Mango (1985) 51, suggests that the population peaked between 300,000 and 400,000 residents, and Morrisson and Sodini (2002) 174, that the population at the beginning of the sixth century was 400,000 or slightly more. With this rapid growth rate late Roman Constantinople was comparable to early modern London, whose population grew from 40,000 in 1500 to 575,000 in 1700: see de Vries (1984) 152, 270. Ocean: Theodoret of Cyrrhus, *Epistulae* XV, addressed to Proclus, bishop of Constantinople in the mid-fifth century. Epitaphs of immigrants at Constantinople: Feissel (1995). Widowed cities: Eunapius, *Vitae sophistarum* 462. For the debate over the size of the barbarian groups in the West, see Heather (2009).

These immigrants included municipal notables. Constantine's son Constantius established a new senate at Constantinople, which offered membership to local elites in the eastern provinces. When, for instance, one young man from a notable family in Cappadocia visited in the 350s, he was immediately recruited to stay by being offered public honors, marriage into a distinguished family, and membership in the senate. Many of these recruits were likewise "new men," lacking a distinguished aristocratic pedigree. At Rome some senatorial families still claimed descent from distinguished heroes of the Republic, such as famous generals and famous magistrates. In contrast, the fathers of the new senators at Constantinople included a sausage maker and a bathhouse attendant. During its initial phase of recruitment the size of this eastern senate increased as rapidly as the city's population. By the later 350s it included about three hundred members, and by the 380s two thousand members. For both municipal notables and ordinary provincials, the boomtown of Constantinople represented "the singing of the Sirens." The opportunities and subsidies at the new capital were just too seductive to resist.[10]

An increasing population needed food and water. Some grain came from nearby regions, such as Thrace in northern Greece and Bithynia and Phrygia in Asia Minor. Most came from overseas. After the establishment of the kingdom of the Vandals in the fifth century, North Africa had no longer supplied grain to Rome; but a century later, after the emperor Justinian's army defeated the Vandals, it shipped some grain to Constantinople. By far the most important source of grain was Egypt. "The fields of Egypt yielded to the empire of new [Rome]." The grain that had once gone to Rome was now diverted to Constantinople; by the mid-sixth

---

[10] Visit by Caesarius, brother of Gregory of Nazianzus: Gregory of Nazianzus, *Orationes* 7.8, with Van Dam (2003) 60–65. Pedigrees at Rome: Jerome, *Epistulae* 108.1, 3, on Paula and her mother, Blesilla, linking them with the families of the Scipiones and Gracchi. Pedigrees at Constantinople: Libanius, *Orationes* 42.24, on Philippus, consul in 348, and Datianus, consul in 358. Increase in size: Themistius, *Orationes* 34.13. Singing of Sirens: Basil, *Epistulae* 1.

century, in fact, more Egyptian grain was being shipped to Constantinople than had previously been shipped to Rome. One observer thought that so many ships were now sailing between Egypt and Constantinople that the sea looked like dry land. To receive these supplies, emperors expanded the port facilities along both the Sea of Marmara and the inlet of the Golden Horn, which eventually included two and one-half miles of docks with berths for perhaps five hundred midsized ships. To store the grain they constructed granaries, including a large one on the island of Tenedos at the mouth of the Hellespont that was half the size of a modern football field. Emperors understood all too well the importance of an adequate supply of grain. When they inspected the granaries near the harbors in the capital, the ceremonial visit was as solemn and elaborate as any high liturgy. And if they had doubts about the capacity of a warehouse, a nervous architect would measure its true dimensions on the spot.[11]

In addition to grain, other sorts of food came from various provinces. According to one historian, from the beginning the new capital had a prior claim on food and other supplies. "Constantine exhausted nearly all the imperial resources on Constantinople." Just as the requirements of Rome had imposed more demands for increasing agricultural production in the provinces, likewise the requirements of Constantinople now affected agricultural regimes in eastern provinces. Some communities were obliged to increase

---

[11] Grain from Thrace: Themistius, *Orationes* 27.336d; from Bithynia and Phrygia: Procopius, *Anecdota* 22.17–18. Egypt: Claudian, *De bello Gildonico* 1.61–62, "Aegyptia rura | in partem cessere novae." According to *Epitome de Caesaribus* 1.6, Egypt shipped 20 million *modii* (almost 150,000 tons) of grain to Rome in the time of Augustus (probably an overstatement). According to Justinian, *Edicta* 13.8, Egypt shipped 8 million *artabae* of grain to Constantinople; this amount is calculated as 36 million *modii* by Garnsey (1988) 231, and Haas (1997) 42, as 27 million *modii* by Jones (1964) 698, and as 24 million *modii* by Durliat (1990) 257–65. Ships: Theophylact Simocatta, *Historiae* 2.14.7, with Durliat (1990) 185–278, (1995), on the grain supply. Docks: Mango (1985) 38–40. Granary at Tenedos: Procopius, *Aedificia* 5.1.7–16. Imperial inspection: Constantine VII Porphyrogenitus, *De ceremoniis* 2.51, with M. M. Mango (2000) 192–94, for warehouses and bakeries at Constantinople.

their production. In Egypt, for instance, landowners invested in various techniques of irrigation; the production of olive oil and wine in northern Syria increased considerably during the fourth, fifth, and sixth centuries; in southern and southeastern Asia Minor there was a significant expansion in the production of olive oil, even replacing other crops. In contrast, provincial communities sometimes suffered because of the inflexibility of the demands. Even in Egypt small villages with variable production were increasingly abandoned.[12]

The supply of water was an ongoing concern. The aqueduct constructed by the emperor Hadrian in the early second century was soon inadequate for a growing population, especially after the emperor Constantius built a new large public bath. In the later fourth century the emperor Valens finally completed a magnificent new aqueduct, which brought water over one hundred miles from the Thracian forests through tunnels and over archways. Even a preacher who had rejected the emperor's theology was impressed by "this unbelievable project, a river that is both underground and high in the air." Complementing these aqueducts was a series of large reservoirs and covered cisterns, which could compensate for the dry summer months and for enemy sieges. Constantinople had more reservoirs and cisterns than any other ancient city. One vast underground cistern constructed by the emperor Justinian was supported by a forest of 336 tall columns. Another large reservoir was known as "Abundant Water."[13]

---

[12] Exhausted: *Origo Constantini imperatoris* 6.30, with Hickey (2007) 292, on irrigation in Egypt, Decker (2001), on olive oil and wine from Syria perhaps exported to "the imperial vortex at Constantinople" (83); Mitchell (2005), on olive oil in Asia Minor, where "in parts of the region olive production may have assumed the pattern of monoculture" (100); and Bagnall (1985), on the abandonment of villages in the Fayum.

[13] River: Gregory of Nazianzus, *Orationes* 33.6. Basilica Cistern, now known as the "Underground Palace": Janin (1964) 208–9. "Abundant Water": Socrates, *Historia ecclesiastica* 4.8.8. For the aqueducts and cisterns, see Mango (1995b), and the comprehensive overview in Crow, Bardill, and Bayliss (2008); also Crow (2007) 279, on the scale of the aqueducts, "which in less than a century became as long as the eleven aqueducts of Rome."

The construction of buildings and other monuments could hardly keep up with the population surge. Constantine initiated the construction of a wall on the west side of the city; a century later the emperors built another wall about one mile farther west. This new wall, about four and one-half miles long, doubled the size of the fortified city. Emperors constructed so many magnificent buildings that one orator used the highest compliment possible in the context of Greek mythology: the city was as gorgeous as the girdle of Aphrodite! One monumental focus of Constantine's Constantinople was a large oval forum, "similar to the Ocean," located on the city's primary boulevard ("Middle Street") and surrounded by a colonnade. In the center of this plaza a huge bronze statue of the emperor presided from the top of a tall column. At the end of the fourth century Theodosius added a new forum farther west, which was a deliberate reminder of the great Forum of Trajan at Rome. As a native of Spain, Trajan had been the first emperor of provincial descent; as another native of Spain, Theodosius could now use the resemblance to enhance his own prestige. On the north side of his forum he erected a tall column decorated with a spiral frieze, similar to Trajan's famous column at Rome. In the center of the forum was a large equestrian statue of Theodosius, extending his hand toward the eastern provinces. Early Constantinople was built, in part, in the image of Rome. As a result, at New Rome emperors could still appear to be presiding like true Roman rulers.[14]

But they were not ruling like Republican emperors. Successive emperors gradually transformed the monumental center of the new capital into a stage set for the display of their rulership. Constantine initiated construction of the Great Palace and the adjacent Hippodrome (the equivalent of the Circus Maximus). The palace contained large halls for the reception of embassies

[14] Aphrodite's girdle: Himerius, *Orationes* 41.7. Ocean: *Patria Konstantinoupoleos* 3.11, ed. Preger (1901–1907) 2:218, with Janin (1964) 62–68, forums, 77–82, columns, and Patterson (1992) 215: "The new imperial capital paid tribute to the old."

and the announcement of promotions, as well as ornate banquet rooms. From the palace emperors and their courts could walk directly into the imperial box to watch races and processions in the Hippodrome, which held up to perhaps 300,000 spectators. Since a palace and a circus were the two monuments that characterized imperial capitals, now it was possible for emperors to perform their imperial rule in the appropriate monumental setting. Once the emperors became permanent residents at Constantinople and no longer led military campaigns in person, the ceremonies became more elaborate and choreographed. New emperors were acclaimed in the Hippodrome. In the reception halls of the palace the emperor sat on an elevated throne. Foreign ambassadors were thoroughly intimidated. In the later sixth century an embassy of Avar warriors concluded that "the Roman palace was another heaven."[15]

Senators often participated in these ceremonies. But in contrast to Rome, where the presence of senators conjured up independent memories of the Republic, in these ceremonies at Constantinople the senators were simply part of the imperial entourage, character actors in a performance dominated by emperors as the leading men. Under Justinian, in fact, senators were expected to prostrate themselves on the pavement and kiss the emperor's foot. A mosaic fresco displayed in the vestibule of the palace depicted Justinian surrounded by senators, who were all "happy and smiling as they bestowed on the emperor honors that resembled those of God." Even though the buildings, the institutions, and the senators were similar to those at Rome, there was certainly no attempt to retain the old fiction of emperors who had revived the Republic. Instead, now the ceremonies imagined the emperors to be God's representatives on earth.[16]

---

[15] Capacity of Hippodrome: McCormick (2000) 159, in an excellent overview of court ceremony. Palace: Corripus, *In laudem Iustini* 3.244, with C. Mango (2000), on the development of imperial triumphal ceremonies.

[16] Procopius, *Aedificia* 1.10.18–19, honors, *Anecdota* 30.21–23, kissing the emperor's foot. For the "imperial" senate at Constantinople, see Dagron (1974)

The setting for the performance of emperorship at Constantinople also included churches. The two most famous were the Church of the Holy Apostles and the Church of Holy Wisdom, "Hagia Sophia." Both churches were memorials of the Constantinian dynasty. Constantine or his son Constantius had initiated construction of the Church of the Holy Apostles, and Constantius presided over the dedication of the Church of Holy Wisdom. The Church of Holy Wisdom was rebuilt after a fire in the early fifth century; the Church of Holy Wisdom whose spectacular dome still towers over the modern city's skyline was the third version, constructed by Justinian after another fire in 532. Because of its immense size, magnificent design, and extravagant decoration, this was a very expensive church. Justinian may well have spent on the reconstruction of the Church of Holy Wisdom over three times the cost of the Baths of Caracalla at Rome. But it was also precisely those lavish features that seemed to mark the church as a direct portal between heaven and earth. In the Church of Holy Wisdom, Justinian and his successors could worship beneath "a golden dome suspended from heaven."[17]

At Rome the important early churches were on the edges of the city, just inside the walls or in the suburbs. Through centrifugal force, however, visits by emperors to these churches gradually subverted the traditional ceremonial topography of the capital toward this perimeter and away from the old historical and monumental hub. In contrast, at Constantinople the important churches were in central locations from the beginning. The Church of the Holy Apostles was on the northwestern branch of the central boulevard linking the forums of Theodosius and Constantine with the city center, and the Church of Holy Wisdom was near

209: "le sénat oriental . . . est aussi une pièce essentielle dans l'élaboration de l'idéologie impériale à Byzance."

[17] DeLaine (1997) 219, estimates the cost of the Baths of Caracalla as the equivalent of 12 million *modii* of grain. Morrisson and Sodini (2002) 188, suggest that the cost of the Church of Holy Wisdom was over one million *solidi*; for the argument that one *solidus* would have purchased 40 *modii* of grain, see Jones (1964) 445–47. Dome: Procopius, *Aedificia* 1.1.46.

the palace and the Hippodrome. These and other churches were hence soon included in imperial ceremonies and imperial processions, as emperors celebrated Christian holidays and saints' days: "the imperial calendar was . . . dictated by the liturgical year." Emperors also worshipped weekly in these churches and listened to sermons with the other members of the congregation. In the end, many of them were also buried in the mausoleum adjacent to the Church of the Holy Apostles. According to one preacher, by being buried near the apostles, "the emperors were the doorkeepers for the fishermen."[18]

Like Rome, Constantinople too had been constructed for the display of emperors and their authority. But in contrast to Rome, at Constantinople emperors did not have to deal with extensive past traditions and a cluster of wealthy senators who would pose as the guardians of ancestral customs and political institutions that predated both imperial rule and Christianity. Instead, at the new capital emperors and Christianity had always been dominant. From its foundation Constantinople was designed for the performance of Christian emperorship, not Republican emperorship.

Constantinople also served as an ideological message to provincials about the defense of the eastern empire. As in the early empire, the other large expenditure for eastern emperors was the maintenance of the army. The emperors continued to support a large standing army, including field troops and garrison troops, as well as federates and allies. They continued to initiate military campaigns, even if they did not lead the expeditions in person. They continued to repair roads and construct fortifications, including walls for numerous cities in the Balkans, the Greek peninsula, Asia Minor, North Africa, and Syria, and along the Euphrates River. Even though he himself hardly left Constantinople, Justinian acquired a reputation for strengthening the distant frontiers "with a host of soldiers" and "by constructing

[18] Quotation about imperial calendar from Cameron (1987) 111. Doorkeepers: John Chrysostom, *Contra Iudaeos et gentiles quod Christus sit Deus* 9 (*Patrologia Graeca* 48.825).

garrisons." A historian from Palestine who served in the entourage of a famous general was duly impressed by Justinian's efforts: "he completely restored to the Roman empire the security that had been previously lost."[19]

The imperial court at Constantinople hence wanted to sustain both the troops for military defense and the ideology of safe frontiers, similar to the implicit contract between emperors and provincials in the early empire. Then provincials had subsidized the extravagance of Rome in exchange for peace and security. Now they were supposed to accept the same deal regarding Constantinople. This could be an expensive bargain. Because of the profligate demands of the capital, to some the emperor might appear to be standing in the Bosphorus, sucking up all the water in the Sea of Marmara. Egypt alone may have contributed enough taxes, in both requisitions of grain and payments of gold coins, to feed the residents of Constantinople and pay the salaries of its civil bureaucracy. A rhetorician at Antioch pointedly grumbled about "that city that lives in luxury on the sweat of other cities." But in exchange for stability and security on the frontiers, provincials were nevertheless expected to tolerate and sustain the extravagant size and voracious appetite of the capital. Their tribute was a sign of their compliance. The people of Egypt in particular might have needed a repeated hint. As a reminder of their submission, the rooms of the Great Palace sparkled with the jewels that Cleopatra had long ago presented to Roman rulers. Even the queen of Egypt had been a "supplicant." The glitter of Constantinople was a representation of power and authority.[20]

---

[19] Procopius, *Aedificia* 1.1.11, frontiers, 4.5.8, security.

[20] Vision of Justinian: Procopius, *Anecdota* 19.1–3. For the contribution of Egypt, see Hendy (1985) 172: "it not only provided the prefecture [of the East] with about three-eighths of its budget, but alone could have supported the metropolis." Luxury: Libanius, *Orationes* 1.279. Nor did this resentment toward the demands of Constantinople soften in the smaller Byzantine Empire of the twelfth century: see Hendy (1985) 51–52. Jewels: Corripus, *In laudem Iustini* 3.17, "supplex Cleopatra."

To maintain the preeminence of Rome emperors had resorted to symbolic imperialism, by directing grain and other resources from the provinces to the capital on a massive scale, by encouraging municipal aristocrats and ordinary provincials to migrate to the capital, by extending privileges to the capital and Italy while imposing taxes on the provinces. Even though these burdens had been linked to an ideology of the blessings of Roman rule, their imposition was a reminder to the provincials that once upon a time they had been truly conquered. Constantinople could not fall back on the same historical narrative and allude to the same memories. Armies from Constantinople had never conquered the provinces in the eastern Mediterranean. Instead, for the new capital emperors resorted to symbolic imperialism not as a reminder of past conquest, but as a substitute for the lack of conquest. The supply of grain and other resources, the massive construction projects, the appropriation of statues and monuments, and the relentless immigration of new residents were all meant to convince eastern provincials of their subordination to a capital that in fact had no underlying claim to their assets and their loyalty.

New Histories for a New Capital

Supplying the new capital represented deliberate decisions by emperors, first Constantine, then his successors in the East. Initially these eastern emperors in fact resided for most of their time elsewhere, especially at Antioch conducting campaigns against the Persian Empire on the eastern frontier. Despite their absence, these emperors nevertheless continued to promote the expansion of Constantinople. At the end of the fourth century Theodosius was the first emperor to spend most of his reign at the new capital. Even though he was a native of Spain and apparently did not even know Greek, he too was committed to enhancing Constantinople, in particular with a new forum and statues that glorified himself. As a symbol of the capacity of the Roman Empire for assimilating provincials, during the second century emperors with provincial backgrounds, such as Trajan, had enhanced the monumental center of Rome itself, and in the mid-third century Philip the Arab, an emperor from southern Syria, had presided over the millennial celebration of the old capital's foundation. Now, in reverse, the role of these emperors from western Latin-speaking provinces in contributing to the early expansion of Constantinople during the fourth century seemed to hint at the same possibility of assimilation.[21]

In fact, like these Latin-speaking emperors who ruled over the Greek East, Constantinople too seemed to be somewhat out of place, an artificial capital, an adolescent interloper among the great ancient cities of the East, an unproven overlord with seemingly no legitimacy or justification to preside over these old provinces. To complement its new historical destiny, it needed a corresponding history. One of the great innovations of late antiquity was the rewriting of the history of early antiquity. The history of Rome had to be adjusted to fit its reduced circumstances, while the history of Constantinople had to be adjusted to fit its newly exalted circumstances. The new capital needed a suitable symbolic history to complement and reinforce its symbolic imperialism.[22]

This new history for Constantinople appeared in different media. One was its own monumental profile. Through the construction of new monuments and the appropriation of old monuments from elsewhere, the emperors located their new eastern capital in biblical, Greek, Roman, and ecclesiastical history.

Constantine himself had already imagined Constantinople in a biblical context. He decorated one of the city's forums with "a [statue of] Daniel with the lions, fashioned from bronze and gleaming with gold leaf." Subsequent emperors brought relics of the prophet Samuel from Palestine. Later traditions also claimed that other important relics had been imported, including the ax that Noah had used to build the ark, and some of the crumbs

---

[21] For emperors at Antioch, see Van Dam (2008b). Philip, "an Arab from Trachonitis," a region south of Damascus: Aurelius Victor, *De Caesaribus* 28.1.

[22] See Dagron (1969), for Constantinople as a Latin capital, and Van Dam (2007a) 184–216, for the use of Latin in the Greek East.

from Jesus' miraculous feeding of the multitude. These two relics in particular had a special significance for a city that was filled with nonstop construction and concerned about the supply of food. In addition, the combination of all these relics neatly provided Constantinople with a place in biblical history. In the process of appropriating the relics, the city had also appropriated their historical significance.[23]

Constantine also initiated the process of inserting Constantinople into mainstream Greek history by importing "famous bronze monuments" from shrines throughout the eastern provinces. These dedications included a statue of Zeus from Dodona in Epirus, a statue of Athena from a sanctuary in Lindos, and a group of statues of the Muses from a sanctuary in Thessaly. The impressively large statue of Zeus from Olympia was likewise moved to Constantinople. Rome had monuments that supposedly rivaled the Seven Wonders of the ancient world; this statue of Zeus was one of the actual Seven Wonders. Another important bronze monument was the tall column of three twisted serpents that the Greeks had dedicated in the Temple of Apollo at Delphi to commemorate their decisive victory over the Persians at the battle of Plataea in 479 B.C. Since at the end of his reign Constantine was planning an expedition against the Persian Empire, perhaps he now saw himself as the new champion of the Greeks. As a result, in the same way that the emperor found a precedent for his military campaigns in Greek history, the presence of these statues in the Hippodrome, before the senate house, or in the palace confirmed the place of Constantinople in Greek civilization.[24]

Constantinople furthermore assumed a role in Roman history. Augustus had marked his consolidation of imperial power

---

[23] Daniel: Eusebius, *Vita Constantini* 3.49. Samuel: Jerome, *Contra Vigilantium* 5 (*Patrologia Latina* 23.343C–D), and *Chronicon Paschale* s.a. 406. Ax and crumbs: *Vita Constantini*, ed. Guidi (1907) 337.

[24] Eusebius, *Vita Constantini* 3.54.1, monuments, 2, "tripods in Delphi," with Bassett (2004) 150–51, Muses, 151–52, Zeus from Dodona, 188–92, Athena from Lindos, 224–27, serpent column, 238, Zeus from Olympia.

with his victory at Actium in 31 B.C. Afterward he had erected
at Nicopolis, the "city of victory," a bronze statue of a donkey
and his driver, who had portended his victory. Augustus had
always claimed that his victory had been confirmation of the
supremacy of "all of Italy." But centuries later, after his victory
statue had been moved into the Hippodrome at Constantinople,
its presence now associated the beginning of imperial rule with
the new capital. Constantinople was also decorated with statues
removed from cities throughout the eastern provinces. The huge
statue of Constantine on top of a column in his forum was said
to have been brought from Troy or a city in Phrygia and to have
previously represented Apollo in his guise as the sun god. The
equestrian statue of Theodosius in his forum was said to have been
brought from Antioch and had previously represented perhaps a
Hellenistic king or an earlier Roman emperor. As one visitor to
the capital noted, "Constantinople was dedicated by stripping
bare almost all other cities." In the process of stealing their monuments, however, Constantinople also appropriated the histories of
these cities.[25]

   The place of Constantinople in ecclesiastical history reflected
its sudden rise in the ecclesiastical hierarchy. At the ecumenical
council of Nicaea in 325, the bishops had agreed to promote the
rank of Jerusalem. Afterward Constantine himself had enhanced
sacred sites in Palestine by contributing to the construction of
the Church of the Holy Sepulcher at Jerusalem, the Church of
the Nativity at Bethlehem, and the Church of the Ascension at the
Mount of Olives. At the same time, however, he was promoting
his new capital at Constantinople by associating it with reminders
of early Christianity. He may have placed a fragment of the True

---

[25] Monuments: Bassett (2004) 192–203, statue of Constantine, 208–11,
statue of Theodosius, 213, Augustus' statue at Nicopolis, with Cameron and
Herrin (1984) 242–45, on the statue of Constantine and the foundation of
Constantinople. All of Italy: Augustus, *Res gestae* 25.2. Stripping bare: Jerome,
Chronicon s.a. 330, with V. Laurent, in Janin (1964) XIV: "une gigantesque rafle
administrative."

Cross in a giant statue of himself. He constructed a shrine that was to serve as his mausoleum, with a niche for his own sarcophagus surrounded by twelve empty tombs that represented the twelve apostles. This mausoleum was eventually included in the precinct around the Church of the Holy Apostles. His son Constantius subsequently imported relics of the apostle Andrew, the evangelist Luke, and the missionary Timothy. At the end of the fourth century the emperor Theodosius imported the head of John the Baptist. In fact, so many biblical and ecclesiastical relics were moved to Constantinople that it was seen as "New Jerusalem." The Holy Land itself seems to have changed address, from Palestine to Thrace. In addition, although Constantinople was already the political capital in the East, now it was given ecclesiastical primacy too. At an ecumenical council in 381, the bishops hailed the capital as "New Rome" and defined a "seniority of honor" for the city's bishop "second only to the bishop of Rome." In the ecclesiastical hierarchy of the East, Constantinople had been promoted past Alexandria, Antioch, and Jerusalem.[26]

These historical and religious relics had once memorialized great events and important heroes at many cities in the East. But now Constantine and subsequent emperors had appropriated them to decorate the new capital. At Rome, the emperors of late antiquity and their architects had confiscated statues, decorations, and construction materials from earlier monuments in the capital in order to build new monuments honoring their recent achievements. At Constantinople, the emperors and their architects did the same, but on a much larger scale by using cities throughout the eastern Mediterranean as their quarries. Late Roman Constantinople was a "green" capital, much of it constructed from

[26] Promotion of Jerusalem: Council of Nicaea, Canon 7. Churches in Palestine: Van Dam (2007a) 293–305. Statue of Constantine: Socrates, *Historia ecclesiastica* 1.17. Mausoleum: Eusebius, *Vita Constantini* 4.58–60. Relics of Andrew, Luke, Timothy: Burgess (2003). John the Baptist: Sozomen, *Historia ecclesiastica* 7.21. New Rome: Council of Constantinople, Canon 3. New Jerusalem: *Vita Danielis stylitae* 10, with Ousterhout (2006), on the importation of thousands of relics to Constantinople: "much of its sanctity was borrowed" (101).

material recycled from monuments throughout the eastern provinces. Even if emperors and their builders thought of this decoration largely in terms of art and aesthetics, in the process they had
stolen the memories and the histories of these other cities.

Constantinople had become more than simply a museum of
confiscated art. Now it was also a repository of pilfered and reas-
signed historical narratives. In some respects, in fact, these relics
and traditions of the eastern provinces seemed to find their true
historical meaning only at Constantinople. Symeon the Stylite
was the most famous holy man of late antiquity to be buried at
Antioch. When in the mid-fifth century the emperor Leo asked
for his body to be sent to Constantinople, the people of Antioch
refused: "we brought him to be a fortified wall for us." Instead,
they sent relics. If Leo could not have the saint's entire body,
he could still appropriate his significance. Upon the arrival of
the relics, the emperor orchestrated a ceremony that highlighted
himself, the city's bishop, the city's people, and the city's own
resident stylite holy man. The most famous saint of Syria had
been turned into a prop for emphasizing the religious and imperial authority of Constantinople. In the mid-sixth century when
Justinian dedicated his reconstructed version of the Church of
Holy Wisdom, he supposedly hinted at a comparison to the old
Temple at Jerusalem by proclaiming that he had surpassed King
Solomon. One tradition even claimed that Justinian set up a
statue of Solomon nearby, gazing at the church that had exceeded
the size and beauty of his own Temple. Through the appropriation of these monuments and their traditions, through implicit
comparisons and deliberate misstatements, Constantinople and
its grandeur could appear to be the fulfillment of biblical, Greek,
Roman, and ecclesiastical history.[27]

---

[27] Burial of Symeon in the Great Church at Antioch: *The Syriac Life of
Symeon* 126, 128, trans. Doran (1992) 193–94. Arrival of relics and ceremony:
Vita Danielis stylitae 58. Justinian and Solomon: *Narratio de aedificatione
templi S. Sophiae* 27, ed. Preger (1901–1907) 1:105, with Dagron (1984)
303–9, on the rhetorical theme of surpassing Solomon. Statue of Solomon: *Patria*

World History

Another medium for the articulation of new histories was, of course, literary narratives. During the early sixth century Hesychius of Miletus composed a history of the world organized around the narrative arcs of Troy, Rome, Byzantium, and Constantinople. His account combined fiction with fantasy within a framework of deities, legendary heroes, and historical figures. By presenting the geographical transformation of Byzantium into Constantinople as the proper sequel to the historical transition from Troy to Rome, Hesychius could associate the eastern capital with the grand traditions of Greek culture and Roman rule, but at the same time separate it from the unacceptable institutions and expectations of the Roman Republic. His Constantinople was the heir of Rome, but without inheriting the problematic aspects of the old capital's early history.[28]

Hesychius' first priority was apparently to locate the development of Byzantium in Greek mythology and history. The traditions he recorded often took the form of etymologies, derived, he claimed, from "old poets and historians." According to these accounts, the outlet connecting Byzantium to the Black Sea was named after the Argive princess Io, who was changed into a cow (*bous*) after losing her virginity to Zeus: hence "Bosphorus," "cow crossing." The city itself was founded by, and named after, Byzas, the leader of settlers from Megara who was also a son of Poseidon and a grandson of Zeus. Byzas eventually defeated a Thracian ruler named Haemus, whose name was attached to the

---

Konstantinoupoleos 2.40, ed. Preger (1901–1907) 2:171, with Bassett (2004) 155–56, suggesting that the statue had originally been of a classical man of letters.

[28] Description of Hesychius' lost history: Photius, *Bibliotheca* 69. For a discussion of the surviving fragments of Hesychius' universal history, see Dagron (1984) 23–29: Hesychius combined two trajectories, "l'une historique qui menait de Romulus à Constantin en ignorant Byzance, l'autre géographique qui allait de Byzance à Constantinople en ignorant Rome" (24). Editions of the fragments of Hesychius are available in Müller (1851) 145–55, Preger (1901–1907) 1:1–18, and Jacoby (1964) 266–72, no. 390.

mountains north of the city. In Hesychius' narrative Byzantium was literally grounded in Greek mythology.[29]

During his tenure of leadership Byzas was credited with constructing a wall and seven towers at Byzantium. Eventually the city was besieged by "King Philip of the Macedonians," presumably a reference to Philip, the father of Alexander the Great. According to Hesychius' account, Philip would have successfully seized the city during one dark and stormy night, if dogs had not woken up the citizens. The significance of these fanciful stories, of course, was not as descriptive sources, but rather in the implications of their subtexts. Even though he mentioned Greek heroes, Hesychius was representing Byzantium in the image of "older Rome." If Rome had seven famous hills, then Byzantium had seven towers, one of them even named after Hercules, who had long been associated with legends about the foundation of Rome. If the foundation of Rome by the brothers Romulus and Remus had included a legend of fratricide, then the origin of Byzantium included a confrontation between Byzas and his half-brother. The defeat of Philip conjured up another celebrated story about Rome. In 390 B.C. a band of Gauls had entered Rome and was about to seize the Capitoline Hill. Suddenly the sacred geese woke up the city's defenders. If Rome had been saved by honking geese, then Byzantium had been saved by barking dogs. The primary source for these traditions about early Rome was the famous history of Livy, whose narrative had extended from "the foundation of the city" to include both the period of the legendary kings and the Republic. Hesychius' account was now essentially a Greek equivalent of Livy's history, a comparable narrative of the growth of Byzantium from its foundation.[30]

---

[29] Hesychius, *Patria Konstantinoupoleos* 2, poets and historians, 5, Byzas and Megara, 6–8, Io, 9, Poseidon, 17, Haemus.

[30] Hesychius, *Patria Konstantinoupoleos* 13, seven towers, 14, Hercules, 20, half-brother Strombus, 27, Philip, 39, older Rome. Geese at Rome: Livy, *Ab urbe condita* 5.47.4.

One oddity of Hesychius' account, however, is that it included very little actual Roman history. Like other Greek cities, Byzantium too had been "enslaved" by Roman rule and included in the Roman Empire. But only one event about early Roman Byzantium was apparently worth mentioning, the devastating outcome of the civil war eventually won by the emperor Septimius Severus in the late second century. Septimius himself was nevertheless presented as a benefactor, because once he forgave the city for having supported his rival, he constructed a new bath and renovated the Hippodrome. For a brief moment the city had been renamed as Antoninia, after the Severan dynasty. Then it became Constantinople, named after Constantine, who likewise adorned the city by extending the walls, constructing baths, shrines, honorific arches, and an aqueduct, and erecting prominent statues of himself and his mother. Hesychius had provided Constantinople with a "Roman" backstory that included Greek mythology and history, but still virtually no Roman history.[31]

If a distinct Roman history was missing from Hesychius' account, so were traditional Roman institutions. The history of the original seven kings at Rome had eventually become problematic for emperors, since their own similarity to kings seemed to undermine their claim to have restored the Republic. In contrast, according to Hesychius, there had been no kings at ancient Byzantium. Instead, the city's seven early leaders had served only as "generals." The senate also had a reduced role. At Rome emperors had always had to accommodate the prestige of the venerable senate as the guardian of the traditions of the Republic. At Constantinople, however, the new senate had been dependent on emperors from the beginning. The senate seemed to be merely the imperial entourage, now settled permanently in one place. According to Hesychius, Constantine had supposedly even built houses from his own resources and donated them to new senators. As a result, the senate of Constantinople did not

---

[31] Hesychius, *Patria Konstantinoupoleos* 35, slavery, 36–37, Septimius Severus, 38, Antoninia, 39–41, Constantine.

have the same prestige or the same reputation as a repository
of ancient traditions. Constantinople could hence be thought of
as an imperial capital, not a senatorial capital that occasionally
entertained visiting emperors. At the old capital the usual short-
hand for the citizen body was "the senate and people of Rome."
At the new capital it was now "the emperor and the people."
Hesychius hence provided a narrative of the growth of Byzantium
into Constantinople that included no kings, no Republic, and an
attenuated senate. The aspects of Old Roman history that had
been troublesome for emperors were now missing or redefined in
New Roman history.[32]

Thinking with Constantinople

Transforming Constantinople into both a colossal city and the
new imperial capital of the eastern Roman provinces required
a sustained commitment by generations of emperors. Only the
importation of vast resources, the construction of many buildings and monuments, the immigration of so many new residents,
and the invention of satisfactory histories could ensure that
Constantinople had a dominant status in the East. But despite
these advantages, its rise to prominence was certainly not uncon-
tested. In the early fourth century when Constantine was planning to found an eastern capital, and still subsequently over the
next three centuries, other famous cities in the eastern provinces
seemed to have stronger claims to preeminence.

Long ago the two great imperial powers in the western
Mediterranean had been Rome and Carthage. Then armies from
Italy had defeated and destroyed Carthage, and for centuries there
had been no alternative to the supremacy of Rome in the West
until the emergence of imperial residences that were closer to the
northern frontiers. Even though Carthage would again become

---

[32] Hesychius, *Patria Konstantinoupoleos* 39, a tablet engraved with the
names of the generals in the Strategium, 40–41, houses for senators, 42, emperor
and people, with Magdalino (2007) 42–53, on the mansions assigned by emperors to aristocrats.

a large city, with a population of more than 100,000 residents, and was even thought in the later fourth century to rank as the third city in the empire behind only Rome and Constantinople, it was still not imagined as an alternative capital. Instead, since its rehabilitation was a constant reminder of its earlier destruction, it would always be a dependency of Rome. Carthage might again be a rival to the capital, "a Rome, as it were, in the African world," but not a replacement.[33]

In the East, however, there were still other important cities that could be sponsored as better candidates to become the dominant city. Rather than transforming the barren little garrison of Byzantium into a new giant capital, Constantine and subsequent emperors could instead have settled in and promoted a city that was already famous, already developed and perhaps quite large, and already very old. The "mighty beating heart" of an eastern Roman Empire could have been elsewhere than at Constantinople.

One potential capital was Antioch, the usual staging point for campaigns against the Persian Empire. Centuries earlier Antioch had been an important city in the wealthy Hellenistic kingdom of the Seleucids in Syria and Mesopotamia. Back then its population had peaked at between 300,000 and 500,000 inhabitants, and during the Roman period it was still a very large city, with a population of probably about 150,000 residents. Complementing its usefulness as a starting point for military campaigns was the city's importance in early Christian history. At Antioch the supporters of Jesus had first been called Christians, the apostle Peter had (supposedly) served as bishop, and the apostle Paul had resided as a teacher.[34]

[33] Lepelley (1979–1981) 2:48, suggests that the population of Carthage surpassed 100,000 residents during the fourth century. Ranking of Carthage: Ausonius, *Ordo urbium nobilium* 2–3, with the excellent discussion of Miles (2003): "For the educated Roman, Carthage . . . could never be an *altera Roma*" (132). Carthage in Africa: Salvian, *De gubernatione Dei* 7.16.67, "in Africano orbe quasi Romam."

[34] Liebeschuetz (1972) 92–100, suggests that the population of late Roman

Another potential capital was Alexandria, which had once been an exceptionally large city in the wealthy Hellenistic kingdom of the Ptolemies. Under Roman rule it was still a very large city, with a population of perhaps 200,000 residents. Tradition claimed that the apostle Mark had introduced Christianity to Alexandria, and subsequently the city hosted many famous theologians and bishops. Like Antioch, Alexandria already had a prominent place in Greek, Roman, and Christian history.[35]

In the early empire Alexandria and Antioch had indeed been thought of as alternatives to Rome as a capital for the eastern provinces, and some emperors had even considered the possibility of moving. In the early third century, for instance, the two sons of Septimius Severus hoped to resolve their feuding by partitioning the empire, with one planning to establish a new eastern capital at Antioch or Alexandria. In the later empire both cities became rivals to Constantinople, in particular during the initial decades after the foundation of the new eastern capital. During much of the fourth century emperors resided at Antioch in order to campaign on the eastern frontier. But after Valens left Antioch to face the Goths in the Balkans in 378, subsequent emperors established themselves and their courts firmly at Constantinople. At first the leaders of these other large eastern cities continued to honor their distant emperors, even if with a bit of resentment. After Theodosius defeated a usurper in northern Italy in 388, for instance, an embassy from Antioch brought gold crowns to celebrate the victory. The bishop of Alexandria likewise sent gifts to Theodosius at Rome. But since the bishop had initiated his compliments before the final decisive battle, he had also hedged his bet by entrusting his envoy with two congratulatory letters, one addressed to each rival emperor. Then it became increasingly apparent that the emperors were never going to return to the

---

Antioch was between 150,000 and 300,000 residents, and probably closer to 150,000.

[35] Haas (1997) 46–47, suggests that the population of late Roman Alexandria was about 200,000 residents.

eastern frontier. The prominence of Constantinople had shifted the focus of the eastern emperors toward the northern frontiers, and they became eastern emperors who no longer visited the East. Neither Antioch nor Alexandria would again be an imperial residence. As a result, since the palace at Antioch was now abandoned, eventually an elderly ascetic pitched his tent beneath the deserted gateway and started praying.[36]

The debate over the contours of an eastern Roman Empire lingered for centuries, articulated in particular in ecclesiastical affairs and doctrinal disputes. The bishops of other great eastern cities found it difficult to swallow their pride. Sometimes they directly challenged the bishops of Constantinople. The hostility of the bishop of Alexandria contributed to the exile of Bishop John Chrysostom from Constantinople. In the prelude to the councils of Ephesus in 449 and Chalcedon in 451, bishops of Alexandria were able to force the removal of more bishops of Constantinople. At other times they mounted an implicit challenge to the preeminence of Constantinople in their incessant arguments over theology. During the later fifth and sixth centuries the emperors at Constantinople typically supported the doctrines of the Council of Chalcedon. To do so, however, meant making a choice about priorities. Since the council had accepted the writings of Bishop Leo of Rome, the emperors at Constantinople continued to cultivate his successors at Rome. But to the dismay of those bishops of Rome, the emperors also tried to accommodate anti-Chalcedonian (Monophysite) Christians, in particular bishops and churchmen in Syria, Palestine, and Egypt. Disputes over theology were hence a symbolic medium for a larger discourse over the construction of an eastern empire. Reaching out to the bishops of Rome implied

---

[36] Feuding: Herodian, *Historiae* 4.3.7, with Ceaușescu (1976), on Alexandria as an alternative to Rome in the early empire. Embassy from Antioch: Libanius, *Epistulae* 878, with the discussion in Petit (1955) 418–19. Letters of Theophilus of Alexandria: Socrates, *Historia ecclesiastica* 6.2.6–8, and Sozomen, *Historia ecclesiastica* 8.2.17–18. Ascetic at Antioch: John Rufus, *Plerophoriae* 88 (*Patrologia Orientalis* 8:142–44).

an interest in the ancient traditions of Roman history; reaching out to the bishops of Antioch and Alexandria implied a concern about the defense of the eastern frontier and the provision of grain to the capital. As they attempted to find a widely acceptable doctrinal formulation, the emperors at Constantinople swiveled back and forth between looking west and looking south. Ancestral tradition, represented by Rome, seemed to clash with the fundamental need for security on the eastern frontier, represented by Antioch, and for food, represented by Alexandria.[37]

These political disputations (but certainly not the theological controversies) finally reached a resolution when much of the southern half of the eastern empire was lost to invaders. In 540 the Persian king Khusro and his army seized Antioch. Khusro took captives back to Mesopotamia, where he settled them in a new city that included a hippodrome and baths. Since this new city seems to have been designed as an imitation of the original, it was called "Khusro's Antioch." Late Roman emperors had included Antioch in an eastern Mediterranean empire oriented toward Constantinople; this Persian king was instead implying that Antioch, and perhaps all of the Roman Near East, should instead be part of a Middle Eastern empire. In the early seventh century the Persians solidified their claim to the Roman Near East by overrunning Syria, Palestine, and Egypt.[38]

The emperor Heraclius eventually defeated the Persians and recaptured the relic of the True Cross, which he restored to Jerusalem in 630. Heraclius was an eastern emperor who did, finally, visit the East again. His victories were an expression of his commitment to an eastern Roman Empire that still included the entire eastern Mediterranean. During his military campaign he

---

[37] For doctrinal controversies as a symbolic idiom regarding the contours of empire, see Kim (2006), on the fourth century, and Van Dam (2008a), on the fifth and sixth centuries, with Schor (2004), on the involvement of Syrian bishops in these controversies.

[38] Khusro's Antioch: Procopius, *Bella* 2.14.1–4, with Millar (1993) 492, "travel round the Fertile Crescent proper will normally have passed through . . . northern Syria," and Van Dam (2008b) 478–79.

became the first emperor ever to visit Christian Jerusalem, and the first to visit Antioch since the later fourth century. He was also the last emperor to visit the Near East for well over another three centuries. Within a few years Arab armies were attacking both the eastern Roman Empire and the Persian Empire. Soon the Arab caliphate had expanded to include the Roman provinces in Syria, Palestine, and Egypt. The imposition of a new empire transformed the orientation of these former provinces in the eastern Mediterranean. Now that the demands of Constantinople were no longer a priority, farmers might grow other crops. In Egypt, for instance, the cultivation of flax as a cash crop for an expanding textile industry increasingly displaced the production of grain. Cities likewise acquired different identities. In Egypt the Arabs founded a new garrison town to replace Alexandria as the political capital. In Syria, Antioch was no longer an important staging center for military campaigns. Already from the mid-sixth century its population had been diminishing rapidly, following droughts and earthquakes that killed tens of thousands, if not hundreds of thousands of residents. In the caliphate Antioch soon became "a quiet provincial backwater." As a result, under Arab rule ancient cities in the eastern Mediterranean no longer competed with Constantinople for political and ecclesiastical priority, because now they were included in a Middle Eastern empire.[39]

The establishment of the Islamic caliphate also profoundly changed the standing of Constantinople itself. On the one hand the capital was left with no rivals to its preeminence in a diminished Byzantine empire consisting of whatever the emperors could hold in Asia Minor, the Greek peninsula, and the Balkans. On the

[39] For the increasing importance of flax in Egypt under Islamic rule, see Mayerson (1997), "An industrial crop took precedence over a food crop" (204), and Udovitch (1999). Foundation of Fustat in Egypt: Kennedy (1986) 65. Earthquakes at Antioch: John Malalas, *Chronographia* 17.16, claimed that 250,000 people died in the earthquake of 526, Procopius, *Bella* 2.14.6, that 300,000 died; Evagrius, *Historia ecclesiastica* 6.8, claimed that 60,000 people were killed in the earthquake of 588. Quotation about backwater from Kennedy (1992) 182.

other hand this was a hollow victory, since the price was the loss of so much of its overseas supplies. Loaves and fishes: without a miraculous intervention, people had to change their eating habits. Now, to replace the grain that had been a large component of their diet, the people of Constantinople increasingly ate more meat and fish.[40]

Rain

For a brief moment during the sixth century Constantinople was most likely the largest city in the world. Then its population too receded, even more quickly than Rome's size had slipped away. At least 40 percent of the residents of Constantinople may have been lost following the outbreak of plague in the mid-sixth century. By the end of the century the city's population had recovered to perhaps between 300,000 and 500,000 residents, certainly almost entirely through an enormous, perhaps even forced, immigration of new residents. Then the bottom fell out under the weight of recurring outbreaks of plague, earthquakes, fires, and military defeats. The loss of Egypt to first the Persians and then the Arabs dramatically reduced the supply of grain, and in 626 the Avars cut one of the primary aqueducts in Thrace. Less grain, less water, but more deaths: now the residents of Constantinople were expected to pay for their bread; now dry cisterns could be used as cemeteries. In the face of these disasters even emperors sometimes despaired. After the loss of the grain supply from Egypt, Heraclius contemplated moving to North Africa. A century later when facing a possible siege by the Arabs, the emperor Anastasius warned all inhabitants to stockpile their own food for three years or leave the city. During the seventh and eighth centuries the population of the capital may have dropped to as low as 40,000 residents. As a result, according to a bishop of Constantinople, "the city

---

[40] Changes in diet: Morrisson and Sodini (2002) 201: "the role of bread diminished, while that of meat and fish grew"; with Dagron (1995), on fisheries, and Maniatis (2000), on pricing fresh and processed fish.

was almost deserted." In just over a century Constantinople had lost over 90 percent of its population from its peak of 600,000 residents.[41]

Edward Gibbon never visited Constantinople. Even if he had, he would not have found the same sort of evocative ruins and hulking reminders of a lost Roman Empire that so haunted his sightseeing at Rome. After the Ottoman Turks captured Constantinople in 1453, the Church of Holy Wisdom became a mosque. The Mosque of Sultan Mehmet the Conqueror soon replaced the Church of the Holy Apostles, the Blue Mosque eventually replaced the imperial palace, and the Hippodrome became a quarry for the construction of the Blue Mosque. Much of Roman and Christian Constantinople was rebuilt as Turkish and Muslim Istanbul. In the early eighteenth century the Ottoman court returned to Istanbul after an extended absence. The sultans, their relatives, and their court officials quickly initiated the construction of new palaces and waterfront pavilions along the Bosphorus, and through magnificent pageantry they reclaimed their place in urban affairs. "Ottoman court life in the eighteenth century seemed to unfold to the rhythm of banquets, receptions, and festivities." These new buildings were furthermore meant to define the standing of the Ottoman Empire between East and West in the new world order. According to an ode commemorating one imperial pavilion at the Topkapi Palace, "the imperial range of vision is the whole world and all that is in it." If Gibbon had visited, he would have witnessed the expansion and embellishment

---

[41] Population fluctuations: Laiou (2002a) 49, loss of 40 percent; Magdalino (2002) 529, between 300,000 and 500,000 residents in 600, 531, perhaps 70,000 residents in seventh and eighth centuries; Dagron (2002) 398, population of 40,000 or 50,000 residents in seventh and eighth centuries; Mango (1985) 54, no more than 40,000 residents. Payment for bread: *Chronicon Paschale* s.a. 618, 626; for the hardships caused by the loss of Egyptian grain, see Teall (1959), Hendy (1985) 44–54, and Laiou (2002b) 702. Nicephorus, *Breviarium* 8, Heraclius, 49, Anastasius, 67, empty cisterns, 68, almost deserted. Theophanes, *Chronographia* a.m. 6206, Anastasius, 6238, empty cisterns, following an outbreak of the plague in the mid-eighth century.

of a capital city, "like a peacock spreading its tail-feathers," much like Rome in the early empire and Constantinople during late antiquity. In the mid-eighteenth century Istanbul was again the sort of imperial capital to inspire thoughts of "Rise and Vigor," not "Decline and Fall."[42]

Early imperial Rome had represented a commitment to an emperorship that nominally respected the traditions of the Republic and to an empire that focused the resources of the entire Mediterranean on the capital. But with the disappearance of emperors to the frontiers and the rise of Christianity, Rome subsequently survived first as the residence of important senators, then as a leading episcopal see. Imperial Rome briefly became senatorial Rome again, then papal Rome. Constantinople, Second Rome, meanwhile represented a commitment to a Christian emperorship from the beginning and to an eastern Roman Empire that focused the resources of the eastern provinces on the new capital. Then most of the eastern Mediterranean was lost to the Arabs. In both cases the great size of Rome and Constantinople had been the outcome of ideological commitments, not economic rationales. Already in antiquity the economic burden of supplying the demands of Rome in the early empire and Constantinople in the later empire had been a consequence of their symbolic value for defining emperorship and empire. As a result, once the emperors adopted other priorities or simply lost control over resources, "everything became much smaller."[43]

For modern historians Rome and Constantinople can likewise serve as inspiration for thinking about the nature of emperorship and the contours of empire. Gibbon too seems already to have sensed that Rome was good to think with, when he famously

---

[42] See Berger (2000) 168–69, on the sites of the Church of the Holy Apostles and the Mosque of Mehmet (Fatih Mosque), and Inalcik (1969–1970), on the importation of new residents after the conquest of Constantinople. Quotations about Ottoman Istanbul from the lyrical description of Hamadeh (2008) 47, peacock, 53, court life, 184, range of vision.

[43] Quotation from Laiou (2002c) 1146, characterizing the Byzantine economy during the seventh and eighth centuries.

claimed that seeing the ruins of Rome had inspired his historical vision about the demise of the Roman Empire. This story was perhaps not as it seemed, however. Instead, it may have been a perfectly postmodern moment. On the morning of October 15, 1764, it rained at Rome, and Gibbon toured an art collection. On that day he may well have visited the Capitoline Hill and listened to the singing of the friars only in his imagination. These powers of imagination do not detract from Gibbon's genius as a historian; instead, they enhance his accomplishment. All of us modern historians wish that we too might have the talent and the boldness to imagine the ancient past while daydreaming about Rome and Constantinople.[44]

[44] The information about the weather at Rome on October 15 was recorded in the journal of William Guise, Gibbon's traveling companion: see Gibbon (1966) 305, and Craddock (1982) 222–23.

Bibliography

Ades, A. F., and E. L. Glaeser (1995). "Trade and Circuses: Explaining Urban Giants." *Quarterly Journal of Economics* 110:195–227.

Aldrete, G. S. (2007). *Floods of the Tiber in Ancient Rome*. Baltimore.

Andrade, N. J. (2009). *"Imitation Greeks": Being Syrian in the Greco-Roman World (175 BCE–275 CE)*. Ph.D. Dissertation in the Interdepartmental Program in Greek and Roman History at the University of Michigan.

Arce, J. (1999). "El inventario de Roma: *Curiosum y Notitia*." In *The Transformations of* Urbs Roma *in Late Antiquity*, ed. W. V. Harris, pp. 15–22. Journal of Roman Archaeology, Supplementary Series 33. Portsmouth.

Arnold, J. J. (2008). *Theoderic, the Goths, and the Restoration of the Roman Empire*. Ph.D. Dissertation in the Department of History at the University of Michigan.

Bagnall, R. S. (1985). "Agricultural Productivity and Taxation in Later Roman Egypt." *Transactions of the American Philological Association* 115:289–308.

Bang, P. F. (2008). *The Roman Bazaar: A Comparative Study of Trade and Markets in a Tributary Empire*. Cambridge.

Barnish, S. J. B. (1987). "Pigs, Plebeians and *Potentes*: Rome's Economic Hinterland, c. 350–600 A.D." *Papers of the British School at Rome* 55:157–85.

Bassett, S. (2004). *The Urban Image of Late Antique Constantinople.* Cambridge.

Berger, A. (2000). "Streets and Public Spaces in Constantinople." *Dumbarton Oaks Papers* 54:161–72.

Bertrandy, F. (1987). "Remarques sur le commerce des bêtes sauvages entre l'Afrique du Nord et l'Italie (IIe siècle avant J.-C.—IVe siècle après J.-C.)." *Mélanges de l'Ecole française de Rome, Antiquité* 99:211–41.

Bird, H. W. (1993). *The Breviarium ab urbe condita of Eutropius.* Translated Texts for Historians 14. Liverpool.

Braudel, F. (1981). *The Structures of Everyday Life: The Limits of the Possible. Civilization and Capitalism 15th–18th Century, Volume 1,* trans. S. Reynolds. New York.

Brunt, P. A. (1971). *Italian Manpower 225 B.C.—A.D. 14.* Oxford.

———. (1980). "Free Labour and Public Works at Rome." *Journal of Roman Studies* 70:81–100.

Bruun, C. (1991). *The Water Supply of Ancient Rome: A Study of Roman Imperial Administration.* Commentationes Humanarum Litterarum 93. Helsinki.

Burgess, R. W. (2003). "The *Passio S. Artemii*, Philostorgius, and the Dates of the Invention and Translations of the Relics of Sts Andrew and Luke." *Analecta Bollandiana* 121:5–36.

Cagnat, R., ed. (1906–1927). *Inscriptiones Graecae ad Res Romanas Pertinentes*, vols. 1, 3, and 4. Paris.

Cameron, Averil (1987). "The Construction of Court Ritual: The Byzantine *Book of Ceremonies*." In *Rituals of Royalty: Power and Ceremonial in Traditional Societies*, ed. D. Cannadine and S. Price, pp. 106–36. Past and Present Publications. Cambridge.

Cameron, Averil, and J. Herrin, with Alan Cameron, R. Cormack, and C. Roueché (1984). *Constantinople in the Early Eighth Century: The Parastaseis Syntomoi Chronikai.* Columbia Studies in the Classical Tradition 10. Leiden.

Campbell, B. (2005). "The Army." In *The Cambridge Ancient History, Second Edition, Volume XII: The Crisis of Empire, A.D. 193–337*, ed. A. K. Bowman, P. Garnsey, and A. Cameron, pp. 110–30. Cambridge.

Ceauşescu, P. (1976). "Altera Roma: Histoire d'une folie politique." *Historia* 25:79–108.

Chenault, R. R. (2008). *Rome without Emperors: The Revival of a Senatorial City in the Fourth Century CE*. Ph.D. Dissertation in the Interdepartmental Program in Greek and Roman History at the University of Michigan.

Christian, D. (2004). *Maps of Time: An Introduction to Big History*. Berkeley.

Christie, N. (2000). "Lost Glories? Rome at the End of Empire." In *Ancient Rome: The Archaeology of the Eternal City*, ed. J. Coulston and H. Dodge, pp. 306–31. Oxford University School of Archaeology, Monograph 54. Oxford.

———. (2006). *From Constantine to Charlemagne: An Archaeology of Italy, AD 300–800*. Aldershot.

Coarelli, F. (2007). *Rome and Environs: An Archaeological Guide*, trans. J. J. Clauss and D. P. Harmon. Berkeley.

Coleman, K. (2000). "Entertaining Rome." In *Ancient Rome: The Archaeology of the Eternal City*, ed. J. Coulston and H. Dodge, pp. 210–58. Oxford University School of Archaeology, Monograph 54. Oxford.

Craddock, P. B. (1982). *Young Edward Gibbon: Gentleman of Letters*. Baltimore.

Crow, J. (2007). "The Infrastructure of a Great City: Earth, Walls and Water in Late Antique Constantinople." In *Technology in Transition A.D. 300–650*, ed. L. Lavan, E. Zanini, and A. Sarantis, pp. 251–85. Late Antique Archaeology 4. Leiden.

Crow, J., J. Bardill, and R. Bayliss (2008). *The Water Supply of Byzantine Constantinople*. Journal of Roman Studies, Monograph 11. London.

Curran, J. (2000). *Pagan City and Christian Capital: Rome in the Fourth Century*. Oxford Classical Monographs. Oxford.

Dagron, G. (1969). "Aux origines de la civilisation byzantine: Langue de culture et langue d'Etat." *Revue historique* 241:23–56.

———. (1974). *Naissance d'une capitale: Constantinople et ses institutions de 330 à 451*. Bibliothèque byzantine, Etudes 7. Paris.

———. (1984). *Constantinople imaginaire: Etudes sur le recueil des "Patria."* Bibliothèque byzantine, Etudes 8. Paris.

———. (1995). "Poissons, pêcheurs et poissonniers de Constantinople." In *Constantinople and Its Hinterland: Papers from the Twenty-Seventh*

Spring Symposium of Byzantine Studies, Oxford, April 1993, ed. C. Mango and G. Dagron, with G. Greatrex, pp. 57–73. Society for the Promotion of Byzantine Studies, Publications 3. Aldershot.

———. (2002). "The Urban Economy, Seventh–Twelfth Centuries." In *The Economic History of Byzantium: From the Seventh through the Fifteenth Century*, ed. A. E. Laiou, pp. 393–461. Dumbarton Oaks Studies 39. Washington, D.C.

Decker, M. (2001). "Food for an Empire: Wine and Oil Production in North Syria." In *Economy and Exchange in the East Mediterranean during Late Antiquity: Proceedings of a Conference at Somerville College, Oxford, 29th May, 1999*, ed. S. Kingsley and M. Decker, pp. 69–86. Oxford.

DeLaine, J. (1997). *The Baths of Caracalla: A Study in the Design, Construction, and Economics of Large-Scale Building Projects in Imperial Rome*. Journal of Roman Archaeology, Supplementary Series 25. Portsmouth.

———. (2000). "Building the Eternal City : The Construction Industry of Imperial Rome." In *Ancient Rome: The Archaeology of the Eternal City*, ed. J. Coulston and H. Dodge, pp. 119–41. Oxford University School of Archaeology, Monograph 54. Oxford.

Dodge, H. (2000). "'Greater Than the Pyramids': The Water Supply of Ancient Rome." In *Ancient Rome: The Archaeology of the Eternal City*, ed. J. Coulston and H. Dodge, pp. 166–209. Oxford University School of Archaeology, Monograph 54. Oxford.

Dolbeau, F., ed. (1996). *Augustin d'Hippone, Vingt-six sermons au peuple d'Afrique*. Collection des Etudes augustiniennes, Série antiquité 147. Paris.

Doran, R., trans. (1992). *The Lives of Simeon Stylites*. Cistercian Studies Series 112. Kalamazoo.

Drinkwater, J. F. (1987). *The Gallic Empire: Separatism and Continuity in the North-Western Provinces of the Roman Empire A.D. 260–274*. Historia Einzelschriften 52. Stuttgart.

Duncan-Jones, R. P. (1982). *The Economy of the Roman Empire: Quantitative Studies*. 2nd ed. Cambridge.

Durliat, J. (1990). *De la ville antique à la ville byzantine: Le problème des subsistances*. Collection de l'Ecole française de Rome 136. Paris and Rome.

———. (1995). "L'approvisionnement de Constantinople." In *Constantinople and Its Hinterland: Papers from the Twenty-Seventh Spring*

Symposium of Byzantine Studies, Oxford, April 1993, ed. C. Mango and G. Dagron, with G. Greatrex, pp. 19–33. Society for the Promotion of Byzantine Studies, Publications 3. Aldershot.

Edwards, C. (1996). *Writing Rome: Textual Approaches to the City.* Cambridge.

Edwards, C., and G. Woolf (2003). "Cosmopolis: Rome as World City." In *Rome the Cosmopolis*, ed. C. Edwards and G. Woolf, pp. 1–20. Cambridge.

Elton, H. (2005). "Military Supply and the South Coast of Anatolia in the Third Century AD." In *Patterns in the Economy of Roman Asia Minor*, ed. S. Mitchell and C. Katsari, pp. 289–304. Swansea.

Erdkamp, P. (2005). *The Grain Market in the Roman Empire: A Social, Political and Economic Study.* Cambridge.

Fant, J. C. (1993). "Ideology, Gift, and Trade: A Distribution Model for the Roman Imperial Marbles." In *The Inscribed Economy: Production and Distribution in the Roman Empire in the Light of* Instrumentum domesticum. *The Proceedings of a Conference Held at the American Academy in Rome on 10–11 January, 1992*, ed. W. V. Harris, pp. 145–70. Journal of Roman Archaeology, Supplementary Series 6. Ann Arbor.

Feissel, D. (1995). "Aspects de l'immigration à Constantinople d'après les épitaphes protobyzantines." In *Constantinople and Its Hinterland: Papers from the Twenty-Seventh Spring Symposium of Byzantine Studies, Oxford, April 1993*, ed. C. Mango and G. Dagron, with G. Greatrex, pp. 367–77. Society for the Promotion of Byzantine Studies, Publications 3. Aldershot.

Finley, M. I. (1985). *The Ancient Economy.* Sather Classical Lectures 43. 2nd ed. Berkeley.

Foss, C. (1995). "Nicomedia and Constantinople." In *Constantinople and Its Hinterland: Papers from the Twenty-Seventh Spring Symposium of Byzantine Studies, Oxford, April 1993*, ed. C. Mango and G. Dagron, with G. Greatrex, pp. 181–90. Society for the Promotion of Byzantine Studies, Publications 3. Aldershot.

Frier, B. W. (2000). "Demography." In *The Cambridge Ancient History, Second Edition, Volume XI: The High Empire, A.D. 70–192*, ed. A. K. Bowman, P. Garnsey, and D. Rathbone, pp. 787–816. Cambridge.

Garnsey, P. (1988). *Famine and Food Supply in the Graeco-Roman World: Responses to Risk and Crisis.* Cambridge.

————. (2000). "The Land." In *The Cambridge Ancient History, Second Edition, Volume XI: The High Empire, A.D. 70–192*, ed. A. K. Bowman, P. Garnsey, and D. Rathbone, pp. 679–709. Cambridge.

Garnsey, P., and R. Saller (1987). *The Roman Empire: Economy, Society and Culture*. Berkeley.

Ghosh, P. (1997). "The Conception of Gibbon's *History*." In *Edward Gibbon and Empire*, ed. R. McKitterick and R. Quinault, pp. 271–316. Cambridge.

Gibbon, E. (1932). *The Decline and Fall of the Roman Empire*, 3 vols. The Modern Library. New York.

————. (1966). *Memoirs of My Life*, ed. G. A. Bonnard. New York.

————. (1984). *Memoirs of My Life*, ed. B. Radice. Harmondsworth.

Gowers, E. (1995). "The Anatomy of Rome from Capitol to Cloaca." *Journal of Roman Studies* 85:23–32.

Guidi, M. (1907). "Un ΒΙΟΣ di Costantino." *Rendiconti della Reale Accademia dei Lincei*, Classe di scienze morali, storiche e filologiche, Serie quinta, 16:304–40, 637–62.

Haas, C. (1997). *Alexandria in Late Antiquity: Topography and Social Conflict*. Baltimore.

Hamadeh, S. (2008). *The City's Pleasures: Istanbul in the Eighteenth Century*. Seattle.

Hamilton, F. J., and E. W. Brooks, trans. (1899). *The Syriac Chronicle Known as That of Zachariah of Mitylene*. London.

Harris, W. V. (2000). "Trade." In *The Cambridge Ancient History, Second Edition, Volume XI: The High Empire, A.D. 70–192*, ed. A. K. Bowman, P. Garnsey, and D. Rathbone, pp. 710–40. Cambridge.

Heather, P. (2009). "Why Did the Barbarian Cross the Rhine?" *Journal of Late Antiquity* 2:3–29.

Hendy, M. F. (1985). *Studies in the Byzantine Monetary Economy c. 300–1450*. Cambridge.

Hermansen, G. (1978). "The Population of Imperial Rome: The Regionaries." *Historia* 27:129–68.

Hickey, T. M. (2007). "Aristocratic Landholding and the Economy of Byzantine Egypt." In *Egypt in the Byzantine World, 300–700*, ed. R. S. Bagnall, pp. 288–308. Cambridge.

Hitchner, R. B. (2002). "Olive Production and the Roman Economy: The Case for Intensive Growth in the Roman Empire." In *The Ancient Economy*, ed. W. Scheidel and S. von Reden, pp. 71–83. Edinburgh Readings on the Ancient World. Edinburgh. Reprinted from *La production du vin et de l'huile en Méditerranée*, ed. M.-C. Amouretti and J.-P. Brun, pp. 499–508. Bulletin de correspondance héllenique, Supplément 26 (1993). Athens.

———. (2005). " 'The Advantages of Wealth and Luxury': The Case for Economic Growth in the Roman Empire." In *The Ancient Economy: Evidence and Models*, ed. J. G. Manning and I. Morris, pp. 207–22. Stanford.

Hoffmann, R. C. (2007). "Footprint Metaphor and Metabolic Realities: Environmental Impacts of Medieval European Cities." In *Natures Past: The Environment and Human History*, ed. P. Squatriti, pp. 288–325. The Comparative Studies in Society and History Book Series. Ann Arbor.

Hopkins, K. (1978). *Conquerors and Slaves: Sociological Studies in Roman History*, vol 1. Cambridge.

———. (1983). "Introduction." In *Trade in the Ancient Economy*, ed. P. Garnsey, K. Hopkins, and C. R. Whittaker, pp. ix–xxv. Berkeley.

———. (2002). "Rome, Taxes, Rents and Trade." In *The Ancient Economy*, ed. W. Scheidel and S. von Reden, pp. 190–230. Edinburgh Readings on the Ancient World. Edinburgh. Reprinted from *Kodai* 6/7 (1995/1996), pp. 41–75.

Inalcik, H. (1969–1970). "The Policy of Mehmed II toward the Greek Population of Istanbul and the Byzantine Buildings of the City." *Dumbarton Oaks Papers* 23:229–49.

Jacoby, F., ed. (1964). *Die Fragmente der griechischen Historiker, Dritter Teil: Geschichte von Staedten und Voelkern (Horographie und Ethnographie). B: Autoren ueber einzelne Staedte (Laender) Nr. 297–607.* Leiden.

Janin, R. (1964). *Constantinople byzantine: Développement urbain et répertoire topographique.* Archives de l'Orient chrétien 4A. 2nd ed. Paris.

Jennison, G. (1937). *Animals for Show and Pleasure in Ancient Rome.* Manchester.

Jones, A. H. M. (1964). *The Later Roman Empire.* Oxford and Norman.

Jongman, W. (2003). "Slavery and the Growth of Rome: The Transformation of Italy in the Second and First Centuries BCE." In *Rome the Cosmopolis*, ed. C. Edwards and G. Woolf, pp. 100–122. Cambridge.

Kennedy, H. (1986). *The Prophet and the Age of the Caliphates: The Islamic Near East from the Sixth to the Eleventh Century.* London.

————. (1992). "Antioch: From Byzantium to Islam and Back Again." In *The City in Late Antiquity*, ed. J. Rich, pp. 181–98. Leicester-Nottingham Studies in Ancient Society 3. London.

Kim, Y. R. (2006). *The Imagined Worlds of Epiphanius of Cyprus*. Ph.D. Dissertation in the Department of History at the University of Michigan.

de Kleijn, G. (2001). *The Water Supply of Ancient Rome: City Area, Water, and Population*. Dutch Monographs on Ancient History and Archaeology 22. Amsterdam.

Kolb, F. (1995). *Rom: Die Geschichte der Stadt in der Antike*. Beck's Historische Bibliothek. Munich.

Krautheimer, R. (1980). *Rome: Profile of a City, 312–1308*. Princeton.

Laiou, A. E. (2002a). "The Human Resources." In *The Economic History of Byzantium: From the Seventh through the Fifteenth Century*, ed. A. E. Laiou, pp. 47–55. Dumbarton Oaks Studies 39. Washington, D.C.

————. (2002b). "Exchange and Trade, Seventh–Twelfth Centuries." In *The Economic History of Byzantium: From the Seventh through the Fifteenth Century*, ed. A. E. Laiou, pp. 697–770. Dumbarton Oaks Studies 39. Washington, D.C.

————. (2002c). "The Byzantine Economy: An Overview." In *The Economic History of Byzantium: From the Seventh through the Fifteenth Century*, ed. A. E. Laiou, pp. 1146–64. Dumbarton Oaks Studies 39. Washington, D.C.

Landers, J. (2003). *The Field and the Forge: Population, Production, and Power in the Pre-Industrial West*. Oxford.

Lenski, N. (2004). "Valens and the Monks: Cudgeling and Conscription as a Means of Social Control." *Dumbarton Oaks Papers* 58:93–117.

Lepelley, C. (1979–1981). *Les cités de l'Afrique romaine au Bas-Empire*, 2 vols. Paris.

Liebeschuetz, J. H. W. G. (1972). *Antioch: City and Imperial Administration in the Later Roman Empire*. Oxford.

————. (2001). "The Uses and Abuses of the Concept of 'Decline' in Later Roman History, or, Was Gibbon Politically Incorrect?" In *Recent Research in Late-Antique Urbanism*, ed. L. Lavan, pp. 233–38. Journal of Roman Archaeology, Supplementary Series 42. Portsmouth.

Lim, R. (1999). "People as Power: Games, Munificence, and Contested Topography." In *The Transformations of* Urbs Roma *in Late Antiquity*, ed. W. V. Harris, pp. 265–81. Journal of Roman Archaeology, Supplementary Series 33. Portsmouth.

Lo Cascio, E. (2006). "Did the Population of Imperial Rome Reproduce Itself." In *Urbanism in the Preindustrial World: Cross-Cultural Approaches*, ed. G. R. Storey, pp. 52–68. Tuscaloosa.

———. (2007). "The Early Roman Empire: The State and the Economy." In *The Cambridge Economic History of the Greco-Roman World*, ed. W. Scheidel, I. Morris, and R. Saller, pp. 619–47. Cambridge.

Luce, T. J. (1990). "Livy, Augustus, and the Forum Augustum." In *Between Republic and Empire: Interpretations of Augustus and His Principate*, ed. K. A. Raaflaub and M. Toher, pp. 123–38. Berkeley.

MacMullen, R. (1980). "How Big Was the Roman Imperial Army?" *Klio* 62:451–60.

Magdalino, P. (2002). "Medieval Constantinople: Built Environment and Urban Development." In *The Economic History of Byzantium: From the Seventh through the Fifteenth Century*, ed. A. E. Laiou, pp. 529–37. Dumbarton Oaks Studies 39. Washington, D.C.

———. (2007). "Medieval Constantinople." In P. Magdalino, *Studies on the History and Topography of Byzantine Constantinople*, Chapter I. Aldershot. Translation of P. Magdalino, *Constantinople médiévale: Etudes sur l'évolution des structures urbaines*. Travaux et Mémoires, Monographies 9 (1996). Paris.

Malkin, I., and N. Shmueli (1988). "The 'City of the Blind' and the Founding of Byzantium." *Mediterranean Historical Review* 3:21–36.

Mango, C. (1985). *Le développement urbain de Constantinople (IVe–VIIe siècles)*. Travaux et Mémoires, Monographies 2. Paris.

———. (1995a). "Introduction." In *Constantinople and Its Hinterland: Papers from the Twenty-Seventh Spring Symposium of Byzantine Studies, Oxford, April 1993*, ed. C. Mango and G. Dagron, with G. Greatrex, pp. 1–6. Society for the Promotion of Byzantine Studies, Publications 3. Aldershot.

———. (1995b). "The Water Supply of Constantinople." In *Constantinople and Its Hinterland: Papers from the Twenty-Seventh Spring Symposium of Byzantine Studies, Oxford, April 1993*, ed. C. Mango and G. Dagron, with G. Greatrex, pp. 9–18. Society for the Promotion of Byzantine Studies, Publications 3. Aldershot.

————. (2000). "The Triumphal Way of Constantinople and the Golden Gate." *Dumbarton Oaks Papers* 54:173–88.

Mango, M. M. (2000). "The Commercial Map of Constantinople." *Dumbarton Oaks Papers* 54:189–207.

Maniatis, G. C. (2000). "The Organizational Setup and Functioning of the Fish Market in Tenth-Century Constantinople." *Dumbarton Oaks Papers* 54:13–42.

Mattingly, D. J. (1988). "Oil for Export? A Comparison of Libyan, Spanish and Tunisian Olive Oil Production in the Roman Empire." *Journal of Roman Archaeology* 1:33–56.

Mattingly, D. J., and G. Aldrete (2000). "The Feeding of Imperial Rome: The Mechanics of the Food Supply System." In *Ancient Rome: The Archaeology of the Eternal City*, ed. J. Coulston and H. Dodge, pp. 142–65. Oxford University School of Archaeology, Monograph 54. Oxford.

Mayerson, P. (1997). "The Role of Flax in Roman and Fatimid Egypt." *Journal of Near Eastern Studies* 56:201–7.

McCormick, M. (2000). "Emperor and Court." In *The Cambridge Ancient History, Volume XIV: Late Antiquity: Empire and Successors, A.D. 425–600*, ed. A. Cameron, B. Ward-Perkins, and M. Whitby, pp. 135–63. Cambridge.

————. (2001). *Origins of the European Economy: Communications and Commerce, A.D. 300–900*. Cambridge.

Miles, R. (2003). "Rivalling Rome: Carthage." In *Rome the Cosmopolis*, ed. C. Edwards and G. Woolf, pp. 123–46. Cambridge.

Millar, F. (1969). "P. Herennius Dexippus: The Greek World and the Third-Century Invasions." *Journal of Roman Studies* 59:12–29.

————. (1993). *The Roman Near East 31 BC–AD 337*. Cambridge, Mass.

Mitchell, S. (2005). "Olive Cultivation in the Economy of Roman Asia Minor." In *Patterns in the Economy of Roman Asia Minor*, ed. S. Mitchell and C. Katsari, pp. 83–113. Swansea.

Morley, N. (1996). *Metropolis and Hinterland: The City of Rome and the Italian Economy 200 B.C.–A.D. 200*. Cambridge.

————. (2003). "Migration and the Metropolis." In *Rome the Cosmopolis*, ed. C. Edwards and G. Woolf, pp. 147–57. Cambridge.

————. (2007). "The Early Roman Empire: Distribution." In *The Cambridge Economic History of the Greco-Roman World*, ed. W. Scheidel, I. Morris, and R. Saller, pp. 570–91. Cambridge.

Morrisson, C., and J.-P. Sodini (2002). "The Sixth-Century Economy." In *The Economic History of Byzantium: From the Seventh through the Fifteenth Century*, ed. A. E. Laiou, pp. 171–220. Dumbarton Oaks Studies 39. Washington, D.C.

Müller, C., ed. (1851). *Fragmenta historicorum graecorum*, vol. 4. Paris.

Nicholson, O. (1999). "*Civitas quae adhuc sustentat omnia*: Lactantius and the City of Rome." In *The Limits of Ancient Christianity: Essays on Late Antique Thought and Culture in Honor of R. A. Markus*, ed. W. E. Klingshirn and M. Vessey, pp. 7–25. Ann Arbor.

Nordh, A., ed. (1949). *Libellus de regionibus urbis Romae*. Skrifter Utgivna av Svenska Institutet i Rom 3. Lund.

Ousterhout, R. (2006). "Sacred Geography and Holy Cities: Constantinople as Jerusalem." In *Hierotopy: The Creation of Sacred Spaces in Byzantium and Medieval Russia*, ed. A. Lidov, pp. 98–109. Moscow.

Packer, J. E. (2001). *The Forum of Trajan in Rome: A Study of the Monuments in Brief*. Berkeley.

Parkin, T. G. (1992). *Demography and Roman Society*. Baltimore.

Patterson, J. R. (1992). "The City of Rome: From Republic to Empire." *Journal of Roman Studies* 82:186–215.

Petit, P. (1955). *Libanius et la vie municipale à Antioche au IVe siècle après J.-C.* Institut français d'archéologie de Beyrouth, Bibliothèque archéologique et historique 62. Paris.

Pleket, H. W. (1993). "Rome: A Pre-Industrial Megalopolis." In *Megalopolis: The Giant City in History*, ed. T. Barker and A. Sutcliffe, pp. 14–35. New York.

Preger, T., ed. (1901–1907). *Scriptores originum Constantinopolitanarum*, 2 vols. Leipzig.

Rebenich, S. (2009). "Christian Asceticism and Barbarian Incursion: The Making of a Christian Catastrophe." *Journal of Late Antiquity* 2:49–59.

Rickman, G. (1980). *The Corn Supply of Ancient Rome*. Oxford.

Saller, R. P. (1994). *Patriarchy, Property and Death in the Roman Family*. Cambridge Studies in Population, Economy and Society in Past Time 25. Cambridge.

———. (2002). "Framing the Debate over Growth in the Ancient Economy." In *The Ancient Economy*, ed. W. Scheidel and S. von Reden, pp. 251–69. Edinburgh Readings on the Ancient World. Edinburgh.

Salzman, M. R. (1990). *On Roman Time: The Codex-Calendar of 354 and the Rhythms of Urban Life in Late Antiquity*. The Transformation of the Classical Heritage 17. Berkeley.

Sartre, M. (2005). "The Arabs and the Desert Peoples." In *The Cambridge Ancient History, Second Edition, Volume XII: The Crisis of Empire, A.D. 193–337*, ed. A. K. Bowman, P. Garnsey, and A. Cameron, pp. 498–520. Cambridge.

Scheidel, W. (2003). "Germs for Rome." In *Rome the Cosmopolis*, ed. C. Edwards and G. Woolf, pp. 158–76. Cambridge.

———. (2007). "Marriage, Families, and Survival: Demographic Aspects." In *A Companion to the Roman Army*, ed. P. Erdkamp, pp. 417–34. Blackwell Companions to the Ancient World. Oxford.

Schor, A. (2004). *Networks of Faith: Theodoret of Cyrrhus and the Bishops of Roman Syria, 423–451*. Ph.D. Dissertation in the Department of History at the University of Michigan.

Scobie, A. (1986). "Slums, Sanitation, and Mortality in the Roman World." *Klio* 68:399–433.

Sirks, B. (1991). *Food for Rome: The Legal Structure of the Transportation and Processing of Supplies for the Imperial Distributions in Rome and Constantinople*. Studia Amstelodamensia ad epigraphicam, ius antiquum et papyrologicam pertinentia 31. Amsterdam.

Squatriti, P. (2002). "Digging Ditches in Early Medieval Europe." *Past and Present* 176:11–65.

Storey, G. R. (1997). "The Population of Ancient Rome." *Antiquity* 71:966–78.

Swain, S. (1996). *Hellenism and Empire: Language, Classicism, and Power in the Greek World AD 50–250*. Oxford.

Teall, J. L. (1959). "The Grain Supply of the Byzantine Empire, 330–1025." *Dumbarton Oaks Papers* 13:87–139.

Tengström, E. (1974). *Bread for the People: Studies of the Corn-Supply of Rome during the Late Empire*. Acta Instituti Romani Regni Sueciae, series in 8°, 12. Stockholm.

Treggiari, S. M. (1980). "Urban Labour in Rome: *Mercennarii* and *Tabernarii*." In *Non-Slave Labour in the Greco-Roman World*, ed. P. Garnsey, pp. 48–64. Cambridge Philological Society, Supplementary Volume 6. Cambridge.

Trout, D. E. (2003). "Damasus and the Invention of Early Christian Rome." *Journal of Medieval and Early Modern Studies* 33:517–36. Reprinted in *The Cultural Turn in Late Ancient Studies: Gender,*

Asceticism, and Historiography, ed. D. B. Martin and P. C. Miller (2005, Durham), pp. 298–315.

Udovitch, A. L. (1999). "International Trade and the Medieval Egyptian Countryside." In *Agriculture in Egypt from Pharaonic to Modern Times*, ed. A. K. Bowman and E. Rogan, pp. 267–85. Proceedings of the British Academy 96. Oxford.

Van Dam, R. (2002). *Kingdom of Snow: Roman Rule and Greek Culture in Cappadocia*. Philadelphia.

———. (2003). *Families and Friends in Late Roman Cappadocia*. Philadelphia.

———. (2005). "Merovingian Gaul and the Frankish Conquests." In *The New Cambridge Medieval History, Volume I: c. 500–c. 700*, ed. P. Fouracre, pp. 193–231. Cambridge.

———. (2007a). *The Roman Revolution of Constantine*. Cambridge.

———. (2007b). "Bishops and Society." In *The Cambridge History of Christianity, Volume 2: Constantine to c. 600*, ed. A. Casiday and F. W. Norris, pp. 343–66. Cambridge.

———. (2008a). "The East (1): Greece and Asia Minor." In *The Oxford Handbook of Early Christian Studies*, ed. S. A. Harvey and D. G. Hunter, pp. 323–41. Oxford.

———. (2008b). "Imagining an Eastern Roman Empire: A Riot at Antioch in 387 C.E." In *The Sculptural Environment of the Roman Near East: Reflections on Culture, Ideology, and Power*, ed. Y. Z. Eliav, E. A. Friedland, and S. Herbert, pp. 451–81. Interdisciplinary Studies in Ancient Culture and Religion 9. Leiden.

Vollmer, F., and H. Rubenbauer (1926). "Ein verschollenes Grabgedicht aus Trier." *Trierer Zeitschrift* 1:26–30.

de Vries, J. (1984). *European Urbanization 1500–1800*. Cambridge, Mass.

Wallace-Hadrill, A. (2008). *Rome's Cultural Revolution*. Cambridge.

Ward-Perkins, B. (1984). *From Classical Antiquity to the Middle Ages: Urban Public Building in Northern and Central Italy AD 300–850*. Oxford.

———. (2005). *The Fall of Rome and the End of Civilization*. Oxford.

Whitby, M. (2000a). "The Army." In *The Cambridge Ancient History, Volume XIV: Late Antiquity: Empire and Successors, A.D. 425–600*, ed. A. Cameron, B. Ward-Perkins, and M. Whitby, pp. 288–314. Cambridge.

————. (2000b). "Armies and Society in the Later Roman World." In *The Cambridge Ancient History, Volume XIV: Late Antiquity: Empire and Successors, A.D. 425–600*, ed. A. Cameron, B. Ward-Perkins, and M. Whitby, pp. 469–95. Cambridge.

Whittaker, C. R. (1994). *Frontiers of the Roman Empire: A Social and Economic Study.* Baltimore.

————. (2000). "Frontiers." In *The Cambridge Ancient History, Second Edition, Volume XI: The High Empire, A.D. 70–192*, ed. A. K. Bowman, P. Garnsey, and D. Rathbone, pp. 293–319. Cambridge.

Wickham, C. (2005). *Framing the Early Middle Ages: Europe and the Mediterranean 400–800.* Oxford.

Wightman, E. M. (1970). *Roman Trier and the Treveri.* New York.

Woolf, G. (1997). "The Roman Urbanization of the East." In *The Early Roman Empire in the East*, ed. S. E. Alcock, pp. 1–14. Oxbow Monograph 95. Oxford.

Wörrle, M. (1971). "Ägyptisches Getreide für Ephesos." *Chiron* 1:325–40.

————. (2003). "The City of Letters." In *Rome the Cosmopolis*, ed. C. Edwards and G. Woolf, pp. 203–21. Cambridge.

Wrigley, E. A. (1978). "A Simple Model of London's Importance in Changing English Society and Economy 1650–1750." In *Towns in Societies: Essays in Economic History and Historical Sociology*, ed. P. Abrams and E. A. Wrigley, pp. 215–43. Past and Present Publications. Cambridge.

Index

Actium, 65
Aegean Sea, 50–51
Aeneas, 52
Alexander the Great, 51, 69
Alexandria, 18n, 66
  rivalry of, with Constantinople,
  73–76
Ambrose (bishop of Milan),
  38–39
Ammianus Marcellinus (historian
  and soldier), 37–38, 40
Anastasius (emperor), 77
Andrew (apostle), 66
Antioch, 29–30, 32, 61–62,
  65–67
  rivalry of, with Constantinople,
  61, 72–76
Antoninia, 70. *See also*
  Constantinople
Antoninus Pius (emperor), 33
Aphrodite, 57

Apollo, 64–65
Aqua Anio Vetus (at Rome), 11n
Aqua Appia (at Rome), 11n
Aqua Marcia (at Rome), 11n
aqueducts at Rome, 10–12
Arabs, 76–77, 79
Argos, 68
Arles, 48
army: size of, 26–27, 31, 60–61
Asia, 23, 50
Asia Minor, 12, 14, 30, 51–54,
  56, 60, 76
Athena, 64
Athens, 7, 24, 32, 51. *See also*
  Dexippus
Augustus (emperor), 1, 8, 10,
  17–20, 35–36, 41, 52, 64–65
Aurelian (emperor), 25
Aurelian Wall (at Rome), 6
Aurelius Victor (historian), 33–34
Avars, 58, 77

Balkan Mountains, 29–30, 32, 48, 51, 60, 73, 76

Basilica Cistern (at Constantinople), 56n

Baths of Agrippa (at Rome), 11

Baths of Caracalla (at Rome), 11–12, 21, 59

Baths of Decius (at Rome), 11

Baths of Diocletian (at Rome), 21

Baths of Nero (at Rome), 11

Baths of Titus (at Rome), 11

Baths of Trajan (at Rome), 11

Bay of Naples, 9

Bethlehem, 65. *See also* Church of the Nativity

Bithynia, 19, 54

Black Sea, 50–51, 68

Blesilla, 54n

Blue Mosque (at Istanbul), 78

Bosphorus, 51, 61, 68, 78

Britain, 30, 32

Byzantium, 48, 50–52, 68–72. *See also* Constantinople

Byzas, 68–69

Caesarea (in Palestine), 26. *See also* Eusebius

Caesarius, 54n

Calendar of 354, 31n

Capitoline Hill, 39–40, 44–45, 69, 80

Cappadocia, 12, 54

Caracalla (emperor), 25n

Carthage, 8, 10, 36, 41, 71–72. *See also* Hannibal

Chalcedon, 51, 74. *See also* Monophysite Christians

Christianity, 38–39, 72–73
    heresies of, 6
    clergy of, 27

Church of Holy Wisdom (Hagia Sophia, at Constantinople), 59–60, 67, 78

Church of St. Agnes (at Rome), 39

Church of St. John Lateran (at Rome), 39

Church of St. Marcellinus and St. Peter (at Rome), 39

Church of St. Peter (at Rome), 39–40

Church of the Ascension (at Mount of Olives), 65

Church of the Holy Apostles (at Constantinople), 59–60, 66, 78

Church of the Holy Sepulcher (at Jerusalem), 65

Church of the Nativity (at Bethlehem), 65

Cilicia, 22n

Circus Flaminius (at Rome), 6n

Circus Maximus (at Rome), 6, 11–12, 21, 33–34, 36–37, 41, 57

cities: population of, 5, 7–8
    mortality in, 14

Claudius (emperor), 17, 33

Claudius Gothicus (emperor), 52

Cleopatra (queen of Egypt), 61

Colosseum (at Rome), 6, 12, 49

column of Trajan (at Rome), 21, 57

Constans (emperor), 34

Constantine (emperor), 25–26, 29
    visits of, to Rome, 28, 39–40
    and Constantinople, 48, 51–52, 55, 57, 59, 62–66, 70–71

Constantinople, 26n
    foundation of, 50–52

population of, 1, 53–54, 77–78
food and water for, 54–56
as symbolic idiom, 2–3, 60–63,
 71–80
as frontier capital, 29–30, 48
as Antoninia, 70
as New Rome, Second Rome,
 Young Rome, 48, 79
as Third Troy, 52
as New Jerusalem, 66
histories of, 52, 62–71.
See also Basilica Cistern;
 Church of Holy Wisdom;
 Church of the Holy Apostles;
 Forum of Constantine;
 Forum of Theodosius; Great
 Palace; Hippodrome; John
 Chrysostom; Middle Street;
 Proclus; Strategium
Constantinople imaginaire, 2–3
Constantius (emperor), 28–29,
 54, 56, 59, 66

Dacians, 20–21
Dagron, Gilbert, 1–2
Damascus, 63n
Damasus (bishop of Rome), 39
Daniel, 63
Danube River, 30, 32, 48
Datianus (consul), 54n
Delphi, 64
Dexippus (aristocrat at Athens), 32
Dio Chrysostom (orator), 30–31
Diocletian (emperor), 25, 27–29,
 47–48
Dodona, 64

economy, 2, 6–18, 22–24, 42–43,
 54–56, 61–62, 76–77
Egypt, 30, 42, 74–77

grain from, 9, 23, 54–56, 61, 76
animals from, 23.
See also Alexandria; Cleopatra;
 Monophysite Christians;
 Ptolemies
emperorship: and Republic,
 18–20, 28–29, 57, 68–71
and Christianity, 25–26, 58, 60
Ephesus, 23, 74
Epirus, 64
Eunomius (bishop of
 Theodosiopolis), 32n
Euphrates River, 29, 32, 60
Europe, 17, 50
Eusebius (bishop of Caesarea and
 historian), 25–26
Eutropius (historian), 34–35, 40

Forum (at Rome), 17, 49
Forum of Augustus (at Rome), 20
Forum of Constantine (at
 Constantinople), 57, 59, 65
Forum of Nerva (at Rome), 20
Forum of Theodosius (at
 Constantinople), 57, 59, 65
Forum of Trajan (at Rome),
 20–21, 57
Forum of Vespasian (at Rome),
 20
frontiers, 22, 30–33, 41
and alternative capitals, 47–48,
 71–74
Fustat, 76n

Galerius (emperor), 28
Gaul, 10, 22–23, 30, 48, 69
Germans, 22
Germany, 23
Gibbon, Edward, 44–45, 78–80
"Glutton," 10

Golden Horn, 55
Goths, 32, 73
Gracchi, 54n
Gratian (emperor), 29
Great Church (at Antioch), 67n
Great Palace (at Constantinople),
    57–58, 61, 64
Greece, 52, 60, 76
Gregory of Nazianzus (bishop),
    54n

Hadrian (emperor), 56
Haemus (Thracian ruler), 68–69
Hagia Sophia: *see* Church of Holy
    Wisdom
Hannibal (Carthaginian general),
    8, 36, 38
Hellespont, 51, 55
Heraclius (emperor), 75–77
Hercules, 25, 69
Heruls, 32
Hesychius (historian), 68–71
Hierapolis, 15
Hippodrome (at Constantinople),
    57–58, 60, 64–65, 70, 78
Holy Land, 66
Honorius (emperor), 32, 40

Industrial Revolution, 5
Insula Felicles / Insula Felicula (at
    Rome), 6n
Io (princess), 68
Islam, 44, 76
Istanbul, 78–79. *See also* Blue
    Mosque; Constantinople;
    Mosque of Sultan Mehmet the
    Conqueror; Topkapi Palace
Italy, 8, 10, 12, 13n, 14, 16–17,
    23, 28, 30, 32, 36, 41, 48, 53,
    65, 71, 73

Jerome (scholar), 42n
Jerusalem, 65–67, 75–76. *See also*
    Church of the Holy Sepulcher
Jesus Christ, 64, 72
    as analogue of emperor, 26
John the Baptist, 66
John Chrysostom (bishop of
    Constantinople), 74
Jovian (emperor), 35
Julian (emperor), 29, 35
Julius Caesar, 17, 37
Jupiter, 25, 44
Justinian (emperor), 1, 54,
    58–61, 67. *See also* Church of
    Holy Wisdom

Khusro (Persian king), 75
Khusro's Antioch, 75
Krautheimer, Richard, 1–2

Leo (bishop of Rome), 74
Leo (emperor), 67
Libya, 13n
Licinius (emperor), 25n, 51
Lindos, 64
Livy (historian), 35–36, 37n, 41,
    69
Lombards, 1, 30
London, 5, 15n, 24n, 53n
Luke (evangelist), 66

Macedonia, 51, 69. *See also*
    Alexander the Great; Philip
Marble Map (at Rome), 5–6
Marcus Aurelius (emperor), 35
Mark (apostle), 73
Mausoleum of Hadrian, 50
Mediterranean Sea, 16, 23–24,
    41, 48, 71
    integration of, 3, 42–43

Megara, 68
Mesopotamia, 72, 75
Middle Street (at
  Constantinople), 57
Milan, 5, 29, 38. *See also* Ambrose
Miletus, 68
Monophysite Christians, 74
Mosque of Sultan Mehmet the
  Conqueror (at Istanbul), 78
Mount of Olives, 65. *See also*
  Church of the Ascension
Muses, 64

Naples, 5, 9
Neapolis, 52
New Testament, 51
Nicaea, 65
Nicomedia, 48
Nicopolis, 65
Noah, 63
Noricum, 32
North Africa, 9–10, 13n, 15, 23,
  30, 43, 54, 60, 72, 77. *See also*
  Carthage

Ocean, 57
Odenath (dynast at Palmyra),
  31–32
Olympia, 64
Ostia, 21, 48
Ostrogoths, 1, 40, 49–50. *See also*
  Theoderic
Ottoman Turks, 78–79

Palestine, 26, 30, 63, 65–66,
  74–76
Palmyra, 31–32
Paris, 5, 29
Paul (apostle), 51–52, 72
Paula, 54n

Persian Empire, 31–32, 35, 48,
  62, 64, 72, 75–77. *See also*
  Khusro
Peter (apostle), 72
Philip (king of Macedonia), 51, 69
Philip the Arab (emperor), 33, 63
Philippi, 52
Philippus (consul), 54n
Phoenicia, 37
Phrygia, 14, 54, 65
"Piglet," 10
Plataea, 64
Pliny the Younger, 19
Portus, 21
Poseidon, 68
"Pot Belly," 10
Proclus (bishop of
  Constantinople), 53n
Prusias (king of Bithynia), 20n
Ptolemies: kingdom of, 73
Puteoli, 9
Pyrrhus (king of Epirus), 11n

Remus, 69
Republic, 54, 58, 68
  warfare during, 8, 22
  commitment of emperors to,
    18–20, 24–25, 33–39, 70–71.
    See also Rome
Rhine River, 22, 29–31, 48
Rhodes, 30–31
Rhone River, 48
Roma (goddess), 36, 38, 42–43, 47
Roman empire: population of, 14
Rome: as symbolic idiom, 2–3,
  41–43, 62, 79–80
  as Second Troy, 52
  in Republic: wars of, with
    Carthage, 8, 10, 41, 71–72;
    hegemony of, 41; population

of, 1, 8, 17; supply of grain
for, 8. *See also* Aqua Anio
Vetus; Aqua Appia; Aqua
Marcia; Capitoline Hill;
Circus Flaminius; Forum
in early empire: population of,
5, 9n, 17; supply of grain for,
8–9, 13, 21, 23–24, 55; supply of olive oil, pork, and
wine for, 10; aqueducts of,
10–12; entertainments of,
12–13, 33; immigration to,
14, 26–28; as consumer city,
15–16; anniversaries of foundation of, 33. *See also* Baths
of Agrippa; Baths of
Caracalla; Baths of Decius;
Baths of Nero; Baths of
Titus; Baths of Trajan;
Circus Maximus; Colosseum;
column of Trajan; Forum
of Augustus; Forum of
Nerva; Forum of Trajan;
Forum of Vespasian; Marble
Map; Mausoleum of
Hadrian; Temple of Peace
in late empire: population of,
49–50, 53; taxation of, 28;
visits by emperors to,
28–29, 36–38, 59; plundering of, by Visigoths, 1, 42,
47; bishops of, 2, 30, 74–75;
as Christian capital, 39–41,
66; rivalry of, with
Alexandria and Antioch,
72–76. *See also* Baths of
Diocletian; Damasus;
Church of St. Agnes; Church
of St. John Lateran; Church

of St. Marcellinus and St.
Peter; Church of St. Peter;
Leo (bishop of Rome)
Rome imaginaire, 3, 24
Romulus (king and founder of
Rome), 35, 41, 68n, 69

saburrarii, "sand diggers," 16n
Samuel (prophet), 63
"Sausage," 10
Scipiones, 54n
Sea of Marmara, 55, 61
Seleucids: kingdom of, 72
senators: at Rome, 19–20, 25,
34–35, 37
at Constantinople, 58, 70–71.
See also Symmachus
Seneca the Elder, 18
Septimius Severus (emperor), 6n,
12, 13n, 24–25, 51, 70, 73
Serdica (modern Sofia), 29, 32, 48
Seven Wonders, 49, 64
Severinus (monk), 32
Sicily, 9, 41
Sirens, 54
Sirmium, 29, 32
Soissons, 32
Solomon (king), 67
Spain, 10, 12, 23, 30, 57, 62
Sparta, 16
Stilicho (consul), 24n
Strategium (at Constantinople),
71n
Strombus, 69n
Syagrius (aristocrat in Gaul), 32n
symbolic imperialism, 23–24, 32,
62–63
Symeon the Stylite, 67

Symmachus (prefect of Rome), 33n, 36–38, 40
Syria, 22n, 30, 37, 56, 60, 63, 67, 72, 74–76. *See also* Antioch

taxation, 2–3, 13, 16, 23, 28, 32, 49, 61–62
Temple of Peace (at Rome), 5–6
Tenedos, 55
Tetrarchy, 25, 30
Theoderic (king of Ostrogoths), 40–41, 49
Theodosiopolis, 32
Theodosius (emperor), 57, 62–63, 65–66, 73
Theophilus (bishop of Alexandria), 74n
Thessalonica, 29
Thessaly, 23, 64
Thrace, 51, 54, 56, 66, 68, 77
Tiber River, 9, 21, 39
Timothy (missionary), 66

Topkapi Palace (at Istanbul), 78
Trachonitis, 63n
Trajan (emperor), 19–21, 23, 35, 62. *See also* column of Trajan; Forum of Trajan
Trier, 29–32
represented as Amazon warrior, 31
as "Belgian Rome," 48
Trojan War, 52
Troy, 51–52, 65, 68
True Cross, 65–66, 75

Valens (emperor), 28n, 30, 34, 56, 73
Valentinian II (emperor), 38
Valerian (emperor), 32
Vandals, 1, 47, 54
Venice, 5
Visigoths, 1, 42, 47

Zeus, 64, 68